TALES *of the* SELF

Remembering Who You Were Before
Life Told You Who to Be

JORGE ARMENTEROS

Contents

Dedication

To the woman whose quiet courage fills every page of this book,

For more than a decade, you have stood at the center of a life built almost entirely for others—raising three remarkable children on your own, guiding them all the way into college, making sure they had not just what they needed, but every chance to become who they are meant to be. You did this while caring, day after day, for your mother, and still giving your whole heart and energy to a full-time classroom of students who needed your patience, your steadiness, and your belief in them.

There are stories on these pages about people who set themselves aside for a long season so others could thrive. You are living proof of how beautiful and powerful that kind of love can be. You carried it all with grace, with strength, and with kindness that never stopped showing up.

I am so honored to stand beside you. Together now, we stand beside our six children and the families growing from the love you spent years protecting and providing for, and there is no place on earth I would rather be than at your side as we watch their lives unfold.

Today, we step into a new chapter, two of the happiest people alive, together at exactly the time we need each other most. This book is dedicated to you, in awe of the life you have lived, and in gratitude for the life we are building together.

Always and only yours,

Jorge

PART I
WAKING UP

Seeing the Life, you have Been Living

You do not wake up all at once.

You wake up in moments—

a restlessness you cannot explain,

a life that looks right but feels misaligned,

a quiet sense that something essential has gone missing.

This part is about noticing.

Not fixing.

Not changing.

Just seeing clearly—for the first time—

the life you have been living.

and the self you have been leaving out of it.

Introduction

FROM SOCIAL MIRROR TO SELF CHOICE

Most people do not meet themselves directly. They meet reflections. From your earliest moments, you learned about yourself by watching faces. A parent's smile. A teacher's sigh. The way someone's eyes shift when you speak. These became your first mirrors—long before you had words for what was happening.

You figured out, without anyone explaining it, which parts of you made people comfortable. Which parts created distance? Which version of you kept things safe.

Over time, you stopped asking:

"Who am I?"

and began asking:

"What do I need to be to stay connected?"

That question was wisdom when you were small. It helped you survive, belong, stay safe. But somewhere along the way, it took over completely. It replaced something equally important:

"Who am I when nobody is watching, judging, or trying to shape me?"

This is the social mirror—the identity you build based on how others react to you, what they need from you, who they are comfortable with you becoming.

The mirror is not cruel. In many ways, it helps you function. The danger is not that it exists.

The danger is that you forget it is a mirror.

Living Behind Glass.

You can spend an entire life inside that reflection:

Reliable

Productive

Strong

Admired

needed

and quietly disappears inside your own story.

You may wake up with a life that looks correct on paper. Nothing is obviously wrong. The job is solid. The relationships' function. You show up, you manage, you keep things running.

And yet.

There is a restlessness that shows up at odd moments. Envy that surfaces with embarrassing accuracy when you see someone living. Fatigue that sleep cannot touch—the deep exhaustion of existing as a curated version instead of a whole person.

You might find yourself with a beautiful house and an empty feeling inside it. A partner you care about but do not feel truly seen by. Work that pays well but makes your chest heavy every Monday. A life that looks impressive and feels strangely misaligned.

That feeling is not weakness.

It is not ingratitude.

It is recognition.

A deeper part of you, the part that was interrupted, not broken, notices when you are living as a role rather than as a person.

What This Book Is and Is not

This is not a self-improvement book. Self-improvement assumes something is broken and needs repair. That you are the problem that requires fixing.

This book rests on different premises:

You were never broken.

You were interrupted.

Self-realization here is not about building better habits or constructing a shinier identity. It's about the quiet, courageous act of remembering who you were before the world taught you that your authentic self was too much, not enough, too loud, too soft, too ambitious, too uncertain.

It is remembering the person underneath all the editing.

The stories woven through these pages are not dramatic epics about triumph. No one climbs mountains or defeats dragons. There are no orchestral awakenings. Instead, they circle ordinary moments when someone feels the almost imperceptible shift between going through life and actually inhabiting it:

A woman realizes she has been living someone else's carefully planned diorama.

A man sees that the person he admires is showing him something about himself.

A parent understands that taking care of others never requires completely disappearing.

These shifts are rarely loud. They arrive like an overheard sentence that lands unexpectedly true, or a realization that changes the entire room inside you without anyone else knowing anything shifted.

Once you see them, you cannot unsee them.

◆ What You'll Find Here

This book is organized around **nine threshold** moments of recognition that reveal what's been hidden in plain sight. At each threshold, you cross from not-seeing into seeing. From the comfortable blur of being lived by expectation into the clarity of choice.

After the thresholds come **seven principles**. These are not rules or instructions. They are patterns of how to actually live from a different place—not from fear or duty or the need to prove yourself, but from the quieter authority of knowing yourself and choosing yourself anyway.

The structure moves like this: you see what's been happening. You understand the patterns. You practice small daily acts that translate understanding into lived experience. You learn to hold your ground when people resist your change. And slowly, you begin to author your own life instead of inhabiting a script written by everyone else's expectations.

None of this requires you to burn down what you have built or reject everyone you love. You do not need dramatic life restructuring. You simply need one thing: the willingness to tell yourself the truth about where you have been living as a reflection rather than as a choice.

Who Might Recognize Themselves Here

As you read, you may see yourself:

in the person who moves through days without fully deciding anything—just drifting from one obligation to the next

in the one who has become an expert at taking care of everyone while quietly disappearing

in the one who studies people they admire and calls it inspiration, while using it as proof of why they cannot

in the one who has perfected the art of waiting for the right time while the years accumulate

in the one whose body is saying something their mind hasn't wanted to hear

You might feel resistance as you read. Grief might surface. You might feel relief so unexpectedly it catches you off guard. All of these are signs that something true is being recognized.

What Actually Changes a Life

It is not an external rearrangement. It is not getting your circumstances to finally line up correctly. It is not waiting for permission from the right person.

What changes a life is the moment the inner author wakes up and remembers:

I am allowed to decide. I have always been allowed. I just stopped believing it.

Everything in this book is designed to help that author—the one that is you—come back into the page of your everyday life.

You are not here merely to fill a role other people need you to play.

You are not here to keep making yourself smaller, so there is room for everyone else.

You are not here only to manage, survive, and endure until you can finally rest.

You are here to live consciously, with your own consent, completely as yourself.

The people who built you wanted the best for you. The systems that shaped you tried to keep you safe. The reflection you learned to wear served real purposes. You can honor all of that and still choose something different.

You can still choose yourself.

An Invitation Back

This book is an invitation to come back.

Not back to who you were before the world began offering its opinions. That version is gone. You cannot unlearn what you learned.

But back to the one you never stopped being—only stopped choosing.

Back to the part of you that knows what you actually want beneath what you are supposed to want.

Back to participating in your own life instead of watching it happen to you.

Back to the recognition that the deepest, truest part of you has been waiting patiently in your wings all along. Not angry. Not demanding. Simply alive. Simply yours.

It does not ask you to be perfect or to understand everything before you begin. It asks you to be willing to look directly at your own reflection—really look—and ask:

Is this who I choose to be? Or am I living someone else's answer to who I should be?

The difference between those two questions is everything.

Welcome home.

Chapter One

WAKING UP TO YOURSELF

Most people do not wake up because life finally slows down and gives them space. They wake up because something small and inconvenient inside them refuses to stay quiet. An old question returns. A familiar room suddenly feels wrong.

A life that looks "fine" from the outside starts to feel strangely unlivable from the inside.

This first chapter is about noticing that restlessness for what it really is. Not a personality flaw. Not proof that you are ungrateful or broken. But an early signal that the way you have been meeting yourself no longer fits the person you have become.

Here, you will walk through the gap between the life that looks correct on paper and the one that actually feels like yours. You will see how the "social mirror"—all the reactions, expectations, and roles that once kept you safe—can slowly become a kind of glass you live behind. You will begin to recognize the interrupted self beneath that glass: the part of you that never stopped wanting, knowing, and choosing, even when you stopped listening.

Waking up to yourself is not a single dramatic moment. It is a series of quiet realizations that gather weight: *I am more than this role. I am more than this reflection. I am allowed to be in my own life differently.* This chapter is your first step back toward that permission.

The Life That Looks "Correct"

The life that looks "correct" rarely announces that something is wrong.

It usually looks like you did everything you were supposed to do.

You show up. You work hard. You pay the bills. You answer messages, return calls, remember birthdays, and keep the calendar full. From the outside, your life might even be described with words like "stable," "successful," "admirable," and "dependable."

And yet, there are quiet moments when you feel uncertain about how to handle them.

You let out a sigh in the car before entering the house.

Sunday evenings often feel heavier than they should.

The brief envy you feel when someone else changes their life, followed quickly by the thought, "That's not realistic for me."

Nothing is on fire. Nothing is collapsing. You may even feel guilty for wanting anything to be different.

This chapter is about that place—the unsettling space where life looks "correct," but doesn't quite feel like it belongs to you.

It is not here to tell you what to do with that feeling.

It is here to help you recognize it for what it is: a first, quiet signal that something in you is still awake.

◆ When Life Fits but You Do Not

Sarah had the lawn, the garage, the mortgage, and the school district everyone wanted. Two kids. A solid husband. Her trajectory left her parents proud and her college friends envious at reunions.

She had checked every box.

College degree. Career. She had tied the knot with a dependable partner. House in a neighborhood where people waved and knew each other's dogs' names. She had built it all deliberately, brick by careful brick, the way you are supposed to.

But lately, something had started to hum beneath the surface. Not loudly. Not dramatically. Just a persistent low vibration she couldn't quite name.

She'd wake up and the first feeling wasn't anticipation—it was the dull weight of obligation. Coffee tasted like nothing. The news felt distant and irrelevant. She went through her day like someone following stage directions:

pack lunches,

sign forms,

attend meetings where the most heated debate was about the color of the new school mural.

She smiled at her husband when he came home and asked about his day. She listened to quarterly reports and office politics and offered the expected responses. She tucked the kids in, read the same stories, and sang the same songs. And felt, each time, a growing hollowness.

One Tuesday, sorting bills at the kitchen table, she found an old photograph tucked in a forgotten envelope. A backpacking trip from her early twenties. Her hair was a mess, her clothes rumpled, and she was laughing—wild, unrestrained—against a backdrop of snow-capped mountains. She remembered the air. The freedom. She reveled in the excitement of not knowing what lay ahead.

That Sarah had been vibrant. Alive in a way that felt almost reckless.

This Sarah felt muted.

She looked at her reflection in the darkened window above the sink. The lines around her eyes came from smiling, yes, but also from worry. The slight slump in her shoulders wasn't just fatigue—it was the accumulated weight of unspoken expectations.

She had done everything right. Followed all the rules. Built the life she was told would bring happiness.

So why did it feel like she was living inside someone else's meticulously crafted diorama?

◆ When Restlessness Makes No Sense

Restlessness is easy to understand when things are clearly wrong.

If you are in a crisis, a toxic situation, or a state of obvious loss, feeling unsettled makes sense. People understand it. They have empathy for it. So do you.

But there is another kind of restlessness that's harder to name: the kind that appears in a life that's "fine."

You may catch it in small, almost forgettable moments:

You finish a long day and think, "Is this it?" and then immediately feel ungrateful for thinking about it.

You look around your home, your office, or your relationships and feel slightly out of place, as if you have wandered into someone else's story and stayed.

You feel more animated when imagining a different life than when living your own.

This restlessness can be confusing because nothing is catastrophically wrong.

You may tell yourself:

Other people would be grateful for this.

I shouldn't complain.

This is just what adult life feels like.

It's too late to change anything big now.

So instead of listening, you negotiate with the feeling. You try to manage it with busyness, entertainment, productivity, or comparison. You remind yourself of people who have less. You talk yourself back into "fine."

Sarah noticed it in others, too, once she started paying attention. The forced smiles at the grocery store. The weary sighs of parents at the park. The way conversations skirted around anything real, settling instead on superficial pleasantries about the weather and sports scores. Everyone seemed to be playing their part perfectly.

One evening, during a particularly bland dinner conversation about Mark's golf handicap, Sarah heard herself say, "I feel stuck."

Mark blinked, fork halfway to his mouth. "Stuck? What do you mean? We have a great life, Sarah. Everything is... correct."

"I know," she said, voice barely audible. "That's the problem. It's all so correct. And I do not feel anything."

He set down his fork. "Are you unhappy?" The question was poignant, weighted with implications neither of them wanted to examine.

"I do not know," she admitted. The honesty of it was both terrifying and liberating. "I feel like I'm supposed to be happy. I have all the things. But the feeling is not there. It's like I'm performing happiness."

Mark was quiet. He wasn't unkind, but he was a man of logic and order. Sarah's emotional ambiguity was a variable he couldn't compute. "Maybe you are just tired," he suggested, reaching for her hand. His touch felt perfunctory.

But restlessness is rarely the enemy you think it is.

It is often an early signal that a deeper part of you is awake and paying attention.

Restlessness without a clear reason is not proof that you are ungrateful, broken, or incapable of being satisfied.

It is proof that something inside you can still tell the difference between living and going through the motions.

You do not have to act on that knowing yet.

At this threshold, it is enough to stop calling it ingratitude and start calling it information.

◆ The Difference Between Failing and Recognizing

When the life you have doesn't match the life you quietly sense is possible, it is easy to assume you have done something wrong.

If I were more disciplined, I'd be happier.

If I were more grateful, this would feel like enough.

If I were stronger, this restlessness wouldn't bother me.

But there is an important distinction to make at this first threshold: the difference between failing and recognizing.

Failing says, "You had one job—make this life work—and you blew it.

Recognizing it says, "You finally see that the story you are in does not fit who you are becoming.

Those two experiences can feel similar in your body. Your chest tightens. Your stomach sinks. Your mind races to explain, justify, or fix. But they are not the same. One attacks your worth. The other invites your awareness.

You are not failing when you notice the misalignment between your inner life and your outer one.

You are recognizing.

Recognizing is an act of honesty, not betrayal.

It does not mean you hate your life, or that everything has been a lie, or that nothing good has been real. It simply means you are telling the truth about the parts that no longer fit.

Consider how you might talk to a child who has outgrown a favorite jacket.

You would not say, "If you tried harder, this would still fit."

You would say, "You grew. That's what's supposed to happen. It's time for something that matches who you are now."

Restlessness can be the emotional equivalent of tight sleeves and a zipper that won't close.

Not a verdict. A sign.

The next day, Sarah found herself driving not to the grocery store but toward the old hiking trails at the edge of town. She parked and walked, her sensible shoes crunching on gravel. The air was cool. The scent of pine filled her lungs. As she climbed, familiar anxieties began to recede, replaced by the steady rhythm of breath and the crunch of leaves underfoot.

She reached a clearing with a panoramic view. Below, her town was a neat grid of houses, a miniature replica of the life she'd built. But from up here, it looked small. Contained.

She thought about the photograph again. That girl had been pursuing something real, something that made her heart sing, even if it was messy and uncertain.

"What do you want?" she asked the wind. Her voice was small but clear.

There was no immediate answer. But as she sat there, feeling sun on her face, a faint, almost forgotten desire began to stir. It wasn't a grand ambition. Not a dramatic career change or a complete upheaval. It was simpler.

She missed creating. She used to paint, sketch, and write stories that lived only in her imagination. Life had demanded practicality, and art had been filed away as a luxury, a childhood indulgence.

She realized the "correct" life wasn't inherently wrong. But it had become a cage built by her own hands and the expectations of others. The bars were invisible, forged from routine and the fear of disruption.

The question is not, "How did I fail to be satisfied with this?"

The question is, "What am I finally able to admit to myself about this?"

The moment you allow yourself to see restlessness as recognition instead of personal failure, the tone of your inner dialogue begins to change. You move from accusation to curiosity. From "What's wrong with me?" to "What is my life trying to tell me?"

That shift does not fix anything overnight.

But it does something quieter and more important: it turns you toward yourself instead of against yourself.

That is the beginning of waking up.

◆ Living as a Role Instead of a Person

Many people do not realize they've begun living as a role until they try to step outside of it.

The reliable one.

The strong one.

The easygoing one.

The overachiever.

The peacemaker.

The one who "always figures it out."

These roles are often formed for good reasons. They helped you belong. They kept you safe. They stabilized situations that would otherwise have felt chaotic or unpredictable. In some seasons, they may even have been necessary.

The problem arises when the role quietly swallows the person.

You might notice this in subtle ways:

You do not ask yourself what you want; you ask what will keep things running smoothly.

You downplay your own needs because "everyone's counting on me."

You feel more comfortable being needed than being known.

When someone asks, "How are you doing?" you answer with how everyone else is doing.

Living as a role feels noble at first. It can even be admired.

You become the one people trust, the one they call, the one they lean on. Your identity gets reinforced every time someone says, "I do not know what we'd do without you," or "You are always so strong," or "You always come through."

But a quiet question starts to surface underneath the praise:

"Would anyone recognize me if I stopped performing this role?"

That question can be terrifying. If your worth has become tangled up in being the dependable one, the strong one, or the uncomplaining one, then changing the role can feel like risking the entire relationship, job, or community.

And so, you keep playing it. Even when it no longer fits. Even when you are tired. Even when a softer voice inside you whispers, "This is not the whole of you."

On her drive home from the trail, Sarah stopped at an art supply store. She felt a tremor of guilt, a voice whispering about wasted time and money. But another voice—quieter, more persistent—urged her forward. She bought a small sketchbook and colored pencils.

That evening, after the children were asleep and Mark was absorbed in a documentary about ancient civilizations, Sarah sat at the kitchen table with the sketchbook open. Her hand trembled as she picked up a pencil. She didn't have a plan, no masterpiece in mind. She just started to draw.

She drew the view from her window—not the perfectly framed, idealized version, but the crooked fence post, the slightly overgrown rose bush. She drew the feeling of the wind, the color of the sky. It wasn't good by any objective standard. The lines were wobbly, the colors muddy. But as she drew, warmth spread through her chest—a flicker of the aliveness she'd felt on that mountain peak.

The first part of waking up is not ripping off the costume.

It is noticing you are wearing one.

You might begin with very small acts of honesty:

Answering, "I'm tired, actually," instead of "I'm fine," to one safe person.

Saying, "I cannot take that on right now," even if you could technically squeeze it in.

Allowing yourself to write down what you want without editing it to be more reasonable or convenient for others.

These are not dramatic rebellions.

They are small acts of remembering: there is a person here, not just a role.

◆ The Beginning of Coming Back

The next few weeks were a quiet revolution. Sarah started waking earlier—not to rush through her morning routine, but to steal an hour for her sketchbook. She slipped out for walks, not just for exercise, but to observe the world with an artist's eye. She began talking to Mark differently, not just about the mundane but about the stirrings within her. He listened, still bewildered, but he listened.

One Saturday, she took her sketchbook to the local park. She sat on a bench sketching the children playing, their uninhibited joy a stark contrast to her former muted existence. A young woman, a stranger, approached.

"That's beautiful," the woman said, gesturing to Sarah's drawing. "You really capture the light."

Sarah felt heat rise in her face. "Thank you. I'm just... finding my way back."

"I know the feeling," the woman replied, a knowing smile crossing her features. "Sometimes the most 'correct' paths lead us furthest from ourselves."

That simple exchange—the acknowledgment from a stranger—was profound validation. Sarah realized the pursuit of a "correct" life, while often well-intentioned, could inadvertently silence the authentic self. The real work wasn't achieving a perfect facade. It was cultivating the messy, imperfect, deeply personal landscape within.

She continued to draw, to paint, and to write. Her life didn't suddenly transform into something unrecognizable. The lawns still needed mowing, and the bills still needed paying. But the hum of discontent had been replaced by a quiet, steady melody of self-discovery. The picture of suburban bliss was still there, but now Sarah was adding her own vibrant, unexpected colors to the canvas, making it truly hers.

The life that looked "correct" was no longer enough. She was beginning to live a life that felt real.

◆ The First Threshold

Drifting happens when you let roles, routines, and expectations make your choices for you.

Waking up begins when you notice that you have been moving more by momentum than by decision, more by expectation than by desire, and more by obligation than by consent.

This chapter is not asking you to burn your life down or walk away from everything you have built.

It is asking you to do something far more radical and far more sustainable:

To tell the truth—to yourself—about where your life looks correct and feels wrong.

Not because you are ungrateful.

Not because you failed.

But because a deeper part of you is finally strong enough to stop living only as a reflection and start living as a person again.

This is the first threshold: noticing that you have been drifting and allowing that awareness to matter.

The Social Mirror

Most people do not start by asking themselves, "Who am I?"

They start by asking, "What do I need to do to stay connected to the people I love?"

Socialization is a double-edged sword. On one side, it gives us language, values, and connection. On the other, it can quietly teach us that love and acceptance are conditional:

Be this, not that.

Achieve this, not that.

Feel this, not that.

Over time, those messages do not just shape our behavior. They shape who we believe ourselves to be.

From your earliest moments, you learn about yourself by watching faces. A parent's smile. A teacher's heavy sigh. The way a sibling's eyes roll. How people laugh or go quiet. These become your first mirrors long before you have language for it. You are already reading the room, already adjusting.

You figure out which parts of you light people up.

Which parts make them uncomfortable or pull away?

No one sits you down and explains this. It just becomes how you navigate survival.

Without realizing it, one question starts to organize everything:

How do I stay loved, safe, and accepted?

That question saved you when you were small. It helped you stay connected to the people you needed. But somewhere along the way, it takes over. It replaces something equally important:

What is actually true about me when nobody's watching, judging, or trying to shape me into something?

This is where the mirror trap starts.

◆ The Earliest Lessons - Before we know who we are, we learn how to be who others need us to be.

Picture a nursery at night. A baby barely able to focus turns toward a sound. Soft babbling. A warm hand. Then a smile so wide it feels like the whole world is saying yes.

The baby doesn't understand words or complex feelings. But it understands: warmth. Safety. You matter. You are welcome exactly like this.

That smile becomes a map, a way to understand the world.

Then the child gets older. Reaches for a toy and meets a frown instead. The adult's mouth gets tight. Something shifts. The child learns fast: some things get approving smiles. Other things get silence or disappointment.

It's not really about the toy. It's about what the world mirrors back when you reach for it.

The child becomes a student of faces. Reading, learning, adjusting.

◆ What You Learn to Turn Up and Turn Down – and How You Start Editing Yourself to Be Accepted

Approval hits often. It's your first trade.

A joke, and everyone laughs. So, you tell more jokes.

A question annoys the adults. So, you stop asking.

Sadness makes people uncomfortable or impatient. So, you learn to hide it, or turn it into humor, or keep quiet.

Being excited gets labeled as dramatic. So, you dim it down.

Slowly—so slowly you do not notice it happening—you start editing yourself.

You turn up the qualities that make people comfortable. You turn down or turn off the ones that seem to create distance or frustration. You are not lying. You are curating. You are trying to be easier to love.

You probably do not remember the exact moments. But you remember the feeling:

The realization that some version of you works better than others.

Keeping peace means keeping parts of yourself tucked away.

The understanding that approval comes from performing, not from being.

In kindergarten, kids laugh together. A little girl on the outside watches them. She wants in so badly it aches. So, she stretches her mouth into the same exaggerated grin. She matches the energy. She performs the belonging.

The laughter includes her for a moment. The relief is incredible. She learns to fit in, even if you have to fake it, and you get to belong.

This kind of self-editing kept you safe in environments that weren't ready for all of you. It protected you from shame or rejection. It even looked like growing up.

But there is a real cost to it:

You start believing that what gets accepted is what's true.

If something in you consistently draws disapproval, you decide it's wrong—not that it's just different, difficult, or misunderstood by people who cannot see it yet.

If something consistently gets praise, you assume it's your most important part—even if it's just a fraction of who you really are.

Piece by piece, you build a version of yourself that works.

And piece by piece, the actual you moves further away.

◆ When You Forget You Are Playing a Role - When the Role Forgets It's a Role

By adolescence, editing becomes invisible. You stop seeing it as editing.

It just becomes who you are.

A teenage boy walks down a hallway. He catches himself in the polished metal of a locker. He studies how his friends move—the way they carry themselves, the expression they wear, the message their posture sends: *I do not care. I'm fine.* It's all a careful construction, but it looks effortless.

He practices it. Adjusts his backpack. Shifts his weight. Practices the unreadable face. The fear underneath—of being seen as awkward, different, weak—drives the whole thing. He's building a mask out of what he thinks will keep him safe.

A young woman sits with her friends while they discuss a show she hasn't watched. She doesn't want to be the one who doesn't know things. So, she offers a vague opinion about the writing, hoping she sounds like she knows what she's talking about.

Nobody questions it. She realizes: to truly fit, she has to be in on what everyone else knows. She has to want what they want, think what they think. Her actual interests have started getting smaller. Her identity becomes a collection of borrowed preferences.

Even as adults, it doesn't stop. A job interview. A first date. A conversation with your parents. Each situation presents a new set of faces expecting something from you.

You learn to perform with confidence when you are not sure.

You adopt interests that match the people you want to connect with.

You say the things that will make someone feel understood or proud or reassured.

You become an actor in every room, adjusting your performance based on the audience.

The original question—"Who am I, really?"—gets buried under a more pressing one: "Who do I have to be to keep things working?"

◆ What Works Versus What's True - "Keeping It Together" Costs You Yourself

At some point, you stop asking *who you are* and start only asking *what works*.

What keeps the peace at home?

What gets me promoted?

What makes my family proud?

What avoids conflict?

What keeps everything running?

These are practical questions. They help you function. They help you survive. But when they become the only questions you ask yourself, something important dies.

"What works" quietly takes the place of "Who am I?"

You can see it in how you make decisions:

You stay in a job that pays well but makes you feel empty every single day.

You keep a relationship that looks fine from the outside but requires you to be smaller, quieter, less yourself to keep it stable.

You say yes to roles and responsibilities that fit the story people have about you—not because they fit who you actually are, but because they fit the role you have been cast in.

"What works" can keep a lot of plates spinning.

It can make your life look successful, stable, even admirable.

But it cannot tell you whether the life you are maintaining actually belongs to you.

You might find yourself defending your choices with logic that feels unshakeable:

"It's a good job."

"They are a good person."

"Most people would be grateful for this."

"It makes sense."

And maybe all of that is true. But underneath the logical defense, something is asking:

"Does this feel like me? Or am I just managing someone else's life?"

That question is risky. It sounds like ungratefulness. It sounds selfish. So, pull yourself back into alignment. You remind yourself of people who have it harder. You convince yourself that this *is* what adulthood looks like.

But the question doesn't go away.

It just waits.

◆ The Limited Mirror - When Feedback Becomes Identity

The mirror itself is not the problem.

You will always see yourself partly through how others respond to you. You exist in relationships, systems, and communities. Other people's perspectives will always matter, to some degree.

The problem is forgetting that what you see reflected is just that, a reflection. Not the truth. Not a verdict on who you actually are.

A mirror can show you:

Which parts of you do people find easy to accept?

Which parts make them uncomfortable?

The roles they've gotten used to you playing.

Which versions of you do they benefit from most?

A mirror cannot show you:

Your full range.

What you actually want underneath the approved version.

What you might be capable of if you weren't performing.

Who could you become if nobody were watching?

When you forget that the mirror is limited, you start treating people's reactions like definitions.

If your boss always praises your productivity, you decide your worth is in what you accomplish. Nothing else.

If your family depends on you to be the stable one, you decide there is no room for your own struggles or breakdowns.

If people laugh at your humor, you hide the serious, grieving, uncertain parts of yourself.

You start living as though the people around you know who you are better than you do.

You might catch yourself thinking:

"If they are disappointed, I must be wrong."

"If they approve, I must be on the right track."

"If nobody gets this desire, it must be foolish."

"If this makes them uncomfortable, I should probably stop wanting it."

But the mirror is only seeing a slice of you. It is seeing what it is capable of seeing. It is not seeing the whole picture.

When you forget that, you hand over your own authority. You let other people's comfort and approval become your GPS. Every reaction changes your direction.

◆ When the Mirror Becomes a Cage - Trapped Inside the Person Others Need You to Be

There were moments when the reflection felt distorted. A sharp comment that stung. A rejection that felt personal and deep. These moments could crack the whole carefully built image.

Sometimes, a small voice inside would stir. A primal instinct to protect yourself. To step back. To say no.

But the habit was stronger. The need to understand what you did wrong and fix it. The urge to adjust your performance for the next person, the next situation, the next chance to get it right.

So, you would analyze the reaction. You would try again. You would be different, better, more careful.

Over time, it becomes such a deep hole that you do not even notice you are in it anymore. You are always scanning the room, trying to read everyone else. Always shifting, adjusting, becoming whatever version of yourself keeps other people comfortable.

And the cost piles up.

You stop knowing what you want.

You lose track of what feels real.

You get really good at taking care of everyone else's feelings, but your own.

Your life looks great from the outside, but on the inside, it is strangely empty.

◆ The Distinction That Changes Everything - What You Learn from Others vs. Who You Really Are

What nobody tells you is that:

You do not need to break the mirror or reject those who reflected back.

You do not have to erase your history or think that everyone who shaped you was wrong.

You have to remember one thing:

The mirror is knowledge. It is not your unique sense of self.

That difference is everything.

The mirror can tell you:

This is how I am being seen.

This is what people are responding to.

This is what's working in this particular system."

But it cannot tell you:

This is who you are.

This is what you should want.

This is the truth about you."

Those are different things entirely.

The moment you separate them—the moment you can see what the mirror is reflecting without believing that reflection is the whole story, something shifts.

You stop playing the role everyone expects from you.

You take a step back toward the real you — the one who has been there all along, watching quietly from the background.

They never disappeared. They were waiting for you to come back.

◆ The Work of This Chapter - Noticing Where You Disappeared — So You Can Begin to Come Back to Yourself

Your job right now is to notice three things:

First: where approval and disappointment trained you to edit yourself. What parts of you learned to hide? What parts learned to perform? When did you stop being you and start being useful?

Second: where "what works" took over from "who am I?" In what areas of your life are you choosing based on what is practical instead of what's true? Where are you maintaining things that work but do not feel like yours?

Third: begin to see the mirror as a perspective, not being imprisoned.

The reactions you get are data. They are useful data. But they are not the definition of you.

This is not about rejecting people who love you or deciding that nothing they've reflected back is real.

It's about beginning to ask yourself the question you set aside so long ago:

Who am I, really?

Not who should I be?

Not who would make everyone comfortable.

Not who fits the story.

Just: who am I?

That question is the beginning of everything that follows.

The Interrupted Self

There is a difference between being broken and being interrupted.

Broken suggests something in you is ruined beyond repair, fundamentally defective, not fit for the life you want.

Interrupted suggests something important began in you—and then had to pause. Not because you were weak or wrong, but because life demanded it.

Most people go through seasons where the self must step aside so that survival, responsibility, or urgency can take the lead. You may have had to grow up quickly, care for others, hold a family together, keep a job, manage a crisis, or build stability from almost nothing. In those seasons, it made sense to postpone specific desires, questions, and parts of yourself.

The problem is not the interruption.

The problem is forgetting that it was meant to be temporary.

When you treat a necessary pause as a permanent verdict, you begin to tell a very painful story about yourself:

"I lost myself."

"I never figured out who I am."

"I missed my chance."

"I do not know how to be that person anymore."

This chapter is about gently rewriting that story.

You were never broken.

You were interrupted.

And the self you think you lost has been closer than you realize.

◆ What Interruption Actually Looks Like

Interruptions rarely announce themselves as interruptions. It arrives dressed as responsibility, necessity, or the only reasonable choice available at the time.

You might have been twenty-three when you put your creative ambitions on hold to take the stable job that would pay off student loans.

You might have been thirty-one when you stopped asking what you wanted because someone else's crisis was louder and more urgent.

You might have been seventeen when a parent's illness required you to become the steady one, the responsible one, the one who didn't get to fall apart.

You might have been forty-two when the relationship that was supposed to support your dreams quietly became the thing you spent all your energy maintaining.

At the time, these choices didn't feel like abandoning yourself. They felt they had to do what had to be done. And in many cases, they were.

The interruption was intelligent. It was adaptive. It kept things functioning when functioning was all that mattered.

But interruptions have a way of extending past their original purpose. What was supposed to be temporary—just until things stabilize, just until the kids are older, just until the debt is paid, just until this season passes—becomes the new normal.

And the self that stepped aside to make room? It doesn't announce its departure. It just quietly moves to the background and waits.

◆ The Story You Talk About What Happened

Years later, when you finally have a moment to look around and realize how far you have drifted from the person you thought you'd become, it's easy to interpret the gap as personal failure.

You look back at the moments when you chose safety over risk, practical over passionate, someone else's needs over your own—and you decide:

"I wasn't brave enough."

"I didn't want it badly enough."

"I'm just not that kind of person."

"I lost myself somewhere along the way, and now it's too late to go back."

This story feels true because it explains the ache. It gives you a reason for why your life looks one way while some other, truer version of it lives only in your daydreams.

But what if the story is wrong?

What if those moments were not proof of your brokenness, but evidence of what you were carrying?

Maybe you took the stable job instead of the risky path because someone depended on you to be steady, and you couldn't afford to fail them.

Maybe you stayed in a role that didn't fit because walking away would have destabilized more than just your life.

Maybe you stopped asking specific questions because there was no safe place to put the answers, no resources to act on them, no margin to absorb the disruption.

In those moments, your system did what it knew how to do: it chose survival, stability, and connection.

It puts certain parts of you on pause to keep the rest of life functioning.

You did not stop being yourself.

You stopped accessing certain parts of yourself.

There is a difference.

And recognizing that difference changes everything.

◆ A Different Question

It can be uncomfortable to admit how much you have set aside. It can feel like weakness to acknowledge how often you chose what was safe over what was true.

But honesty here is not an indictment. It's an act of compassion.

Instead of asking, "Why was I so broken back then?" you might try a different question:

"What was I protecting? What was I holding together? What did that younger version of me not have yet that I have now?"

The answer is rarely "nothing."

More often, it sounds like:

"I didn't have financial stability yet."

"I didn't have support."

"I didn't have permission—from others or from myself."

"I didn't have the awareness I have now."

"I didn't have the luxury of falling apart."

When you look at it this way, the interruption stops looking like failure and starts looking like a strategy. A necessary, intelligent, temporary strategy that kept you alive, connected, and functional during a season when those things were not guaranteed.

The problem is not that you interrupted yourself.

The problem is that you never gave yourself permission to resume.

◆ Where the Self Waits: Daydreams, Journals, and "Someday"

The self you set aside does not disappear.

It relocates.

It moves into places that feel optional, unurgent, and easy to dismiss—places you tell yourself you'll come back to when things "calm down" or "make more sense."

You can often find it hiding in:

Daydreams.

The scenes you replay in your mind when no one needs anything from you. The alternate lives you imagine: different work, a slower pace, a creative pursuit, a conversation you have never been brave enough to have. You call them fantasies or distractions. But often, they are signals—your interrupted self-trying to get your attention through the only channel still open.

Journals and unfinished notes.

The pages where you once wrote honestly—and then closed the notebook because it felt too raw, too unrealistic, or too inconvenient to admit out loud. The sentences that begin with "I wish…" or "If it were only up to me…" or "Someday I want to…" You stopped writing them not because they stopped being true, but because acting on them felt impossible.

"Someday" conversations.

The lines you throw into conversations with friends, half-joking, half-serious: "Someday I'd love to…" "One day when things slow down…" "Maybe in another life I would have…" You say them lightly, as if they do not matter. But your voice knows they do.

Subtle envy.

The lives, choices, or freedoms you envy in others. Not the loud, performative envy of comparison, but the quiet ache when you see someone doing something you told yourself wasn't possible for you, when someone quits their job to travel. When someone goes back to school at forty-five. When someone sets a boundary, you have never allowed yourself to set. The envy tells you: *This matters to me. This is something I want but have convinced myself I cannot have.*

Projects started and abandoned.

The guitar in the closet. The half-written manuscript. The business plan you sketched out and never pursued. The language learning app you used twice and then forgot about.

This is not evidence of your flakiness or lack of follow-through. They are evidence of what has remained alive in you despite everything—trying, over and over, to find a way back into your life.

These are not signs of irresponsibility or inability to "grow up."

They are evidence of what has remained alive in you despite everything.

The self you postponed leaves breadcrumbs. It speaks in almost-whispers: "I'm still here. I haven't gone anywhere. I've just been waiting for conditions that feel safe enough for you to remember me."

◆ Work at This Threshold

The work at this threshold is not to bulldoze your life to chase every daydream.

It is not to quit your job, leave your relationship, or upend everything you have built in pursuit of some romanticized version of your "true self."

The work is more straightforward and more complex:

Stop dismissing these inner signals as childish, foolish, or selfish—and start treating them as data.

◆ You might begin by asking:

Which daydreams have followed me for years?

Not the ones that come and go, but the ones that return consistently, in different forms, across different seasons of life.

What themes keep appearing in my private writing or thoughts?

What do you keep coming back to when you are alone, when no one is listening, when you are not performing for anyone?

What do I keep promising myself I'll come back to "someday"?

What has "someday" been holding for you? And how long has it been holding it?

What envy keeps surfacing, even when I try to talk myself out of it?

Whose life, whose choice, whose freedom makes you feel something sharp and uncomfortable? That sharpness is information.

What part of me have I been treating as optional?

What have you told yourself you can live without, even though it keeps coming back?

You do not need to act on any of this yet.

Remembering is a form of movement.

Simply admitting, "This part of me has been waiting," is a way of turning toward yourself again.

It is the beginning of resuming what was interrupted.

◆ The Body's Truth: Saying Yes While Meaning No

Even when your mind has learned to argue with your desires, rationalize your choices, and override your instincts, your body often refuses to lie.

You can talk yourself into a lot of things:

"It's not that bad."

"This is just what people my age do."

"I should be grateful."

"I do not really need that."

But your body keeps its own record.

You might notice it in:

The way your shoulders tighten every time you agree to something you do not actually have the capacity for.

The fatigue that hits not just after a long day, but specifically after a conversation where you said "yes" while everything in you whispered "no."

The headaches, the knots in your stomach, the shallow breathing that show up around certain people, places, or commitments—even when they "make sense" on paper.

The persistent low-grade anxiety that has no obvious source but never quite goes away, because you are constantly managing the gap between what you are doing and what feels true.

The numbness that settles in when you have been overriding yourself for so long that you have stopped feeling much of anything at all.

Saying yes while meaning no is one of the most common ways the self gets interrupted.

Outwardly, you maintain harmony. You keep things running. You stay connected. You do not make waves.

Inwardly, you begin to fracture.

Part of you is performing an agreement. Part of you is carrying the weight of betrayal—self-betrayal, the kind that accumulates slowly and quietly until you can no longer tell the difference between what you actually want and what you have convinced yourself to want.

This is not always dramatic. It often happens in small, daily moments:

Agreeing to a project you do not have time for because saying no feels uncomfortable.

Saying, "It's fine," when something clearly hurt, because naming the hurt would create conflict.

Telling yourself, "It's not a big deal," about something that feels like a huge deal to your nervous system.

Showing up for plans you do not want to attend because backing out feels selfish.

Staying in conversations that drain you because leaving feels rude.

Over time, these small internal misalignments add up.

You might start to feel inexplicably tired, resentful, or numb. Not because you are broken, but because you are consistently living out of sync with your own consent.

The body becomes the place where the interrupted self tries to speak.

It might say, through tension and exhaustion: "I cannot keep agreeing to things that cost me this much."

It might say, through anxiety: "I do not feel safe in this pattern, even if you keep telling yourself it's normal."

It might say, through a heavy, quiet sadness: "I miss us. I miss you choosing me."

◆ Listening Without Overreacting

Listening to the body's truth is not about dramatizing every discomfort or abandoning every responsibility.

It is not permission to blow up your life every time you feel tired or conflicted.

It is about recognizing that your physical responses often carry information your mind has learned to override.

Your body is not trying to sabotage you. It is trying to protect you—from depletion, from misalignment, from living in a way that is not sustainable.

At this threshold, a few small experiments can begin to reintroduce honesty:

Pause before saying 'yes,' even for three seconds. Notice what your body does when you consider saying yes—and when you imagine saying no. Does your chest open or close? Do your shoulders drop or rise? Does your breath deepen or shallow?

Name your "no" somewhere. If you cannot say it to the person yet, write it in a journal: "I didn't want to say yes to that." Acknowledge the mismatch. Stop pretending it doesn't exist.

Track patterns. Where do you consistently feel heavy, tight, or drained? Where do you feel lighter, calmer, more present—even when the situation is challenging? Your body knows the difference between hard-but-aligned and hard-because-misaligned.

Ask: "What would it cost me to keep ignoring this?" Not just today, but over the next year. The next five years. What does chronic self-override do to a person?

You are not weak for having a body that protests misalignment.

◆ **You are alive.**

And aliveness insists on being honored, even when it's inconvenient.

◆ The Invitation of This Chapter

You were never broken.

You were busy. You were protecting. You were surviving.

You were holding more than most people know.

The self you think you lost has not gone anywhere. It relocated to daydreams, unfinished notebooks, "someday" conversations, and the quiet protests of your own body. It has been waiting—patiently, persistently—for you to remember it exists.

This chapter is not asking you to fix yourself, because you were never broken.

It is asking you to do something both more straightforward and more complex:

Stop telling the interrupted self to be quiet.

Start listening long enough to remember who went silent so that everything else could keep going.

You did not lose yourself.

You put yourself on hold.

And now—right now, in this moment, with everything you have learned and everything you have survived—you have something you didn't have before:

The awareness that the pause was temporary.

The capacity to choose differently.

The permission to pick up where you left off.

This chapter is your permission slip.

The interrupted self is still waiting.

And it's time to let it speak again.

What comes next is not about changing your life yet, but about learning to recognize the landscape you've been moving through.

PART II
CROSSING THE INNER THRESHOLDS

From Noticing to Seeing

There are moments when awareness sharpens and you can no longer pretend you do not see what you see.

This part is about recognition.

About naming patterns without defending them.

About standing at the edge of your own life

and telling the truth about where you are.

Nothing changes here—but everything becomes visible.

Chapter Two

NINE INNER THRESHOLDS

This part of the book is not about fixing your life or optimizing your routines. It is about naming the quiet inner crossings that happen long before anything visible changes.

What a Threshold Is (Not a Plan, But a Recognition)

There are moments in life when nothing on the outside looks different, but something inside quietly refuses to go back to how it was.

No one else may notice.

You still go to work. You still answer messages. You still do what is expected.

But a sentence lands that you cannot un-hear. A feeling surfaces that you cannot push down the way you used to.

A question does not leave, no matter how politely you ignore it.

That is a threshold.

A threshold is not a plan.

It is not a five-step process, a workbook, or a schedule.

A threshold is a moment of recognition you cannot unknow.

It is the instant you realize, "I am not just busy; I am drifting."

The quiet confession, "I am present in this room, but not really here."

The uncomfortable clarity, "I call this admiration, but it might actually be avoidance."

The ache of seeing that "later" has quietly become "never."

On the outside, nothing may change in that moment. On the inside, everything has been rearranged. You may keep doing what you have been doing for a while. But you can no longer do it with the same innocence. You know too much now.

Thresholds are not about effort. They are about honesty. You do not cross them by trying harder. You cross them by telling the truth about where you are.

This chapter is about those inner crossings—about the precise, quiet points where your life begins to turn before any of the visible changes catch up.

The Nine Inner Thresholds (Overview)

What follows are nine inner thresholds—nine distinct moments of recognition that tend to appear when someone starts waking up to their own life. They are not levels to achieve or tasks to complete. They are places to notice.

You may move through them more than once. You may circle back. You may feel several at the same time. That is not a problem; it is simply how real lives unfold.

Here is the terrain you are about to walk through:

- Threshold 1 – Drifting

  The realization that you are moving through your days on automatic, letting habit and momentum decide for you while you are only half present to your own life.

- Threshold 2 – Disappearing

  The recognition that you are physically here but emotionally gone—watching your life from the edges instead of feeling like you are actually in it.

- Threshold 3 – Realizing Admiration Has Become Avoidance

  The moment you see that studying other people's lives, routines, and courage has become a way to delay claiming your own.

- Threshold 4 – Performing

  The awareness that you are playing the role that is expected of you instead of telling the truth—managing your image so well that you start to lose sight of yourself.

- Threshold 5 – Surviving

  The honest admission that you are no longer really living; you are just getting through—on overload, with no space left to ask what you actually want.

- Threshold 6 – Excusing

  The point where the stories you tell about why you cannot change begin to sound rehearsed, and you recognize them as excuses you have outgrown.

- Threshold 7 – The Unshakable Question

  The experience of carrying a question about your life that keeps returning, no matter how you distract yourself, because it is pointing you toward a truth you are meant to face.

- Threshold 8 – Facing the Moment Where Excuses No Longer Fit

  The sober clarity that the reasons you have given yourself for staying the same are not facts about the world but choices you are making—and can choose differently.

- Threshold 9 – Remembering

  The quiet, holy moment when you reconnect with who you really are and can no longer pretend that your life as it is now is the full truth of you.

After these nine, you will come to several key waypoints:

- **How These Thresholds Are Really Crossed** – a short bridge about why effort is not what moves you through, and what actually does.

- **A Life Witness** and **She Came Back to Herself** – a lived story of what it looks like when someone begins to move through these crossings in real time.

- **The Cost of Living on Autopilot** – a warning about what happens when you see clearly and still choose to stay asleep.

- **The Life That Was Waiting** – a closing reflection on the self and the life that have been quietly waiting beneath all your postponements.

How to Use This Chapter

You do not need to "work through" these thresholds in order. Real lives are not organized that neatly.

Some of these thresholds you may have already crossed without having language for them. Others you may sense in the distance, not yet ready to step toward. Some will feel like they were written directly to you. Others may feel less immediate now but become suddenly relevant later.

Let this chapter meet you where you already are.

For each threshold, you will find:

A brief description of the inner moment itself—what it sounds like, feels like, and why it matters.

A small tale or vignette that captures the threshold in motion, so you can feel it rather than just understand it.

A handful of "Questions to Carry with You"—not assignments to complete, but gentle prompts you can hold in the back of your mind as you move through your ordinary days.

You do not have to sit down and answer every question. You can if it helps. But often, the most important work happens when a question lingers quietly and then surfaces later in a conversation, a commute, a sleepless night, or a small decision.

A few ways to move through this chapter:

Read slowly. One threshold at a time is enough. Let it echo for a day or a week before moving on.

Notice resonance. If a line or vignette makes you exhale, bristle, or feel unexpectedly seen, pause there. That reaction is information.

Follow the heat. If one threshold feels especially alive for you right now, you are allowed to stay with it and skip ahead or back as needed.

Most importantly: treat these thresholds as places to notice, not problems to fix.

You are not failing if you recognize yourself in several of them at once. You are not behind if you have crossed some of them before and then forgotten. Recognition is not a test. It is an invitation.

Everything that comes later, the principles, the practices, the daily choices—will grow out of these quiet recognitions. For now, you do not need to know what to do differently. You only need to see, with a little more honesty, where you already are.

Threshold 1 – Noticing You Are Drifting Instead of Deciding

Drifting is moving through your days on automatic, letting habit and momentum decide for you while you are only half present to your own life.

There comes a day when "I do not know, it just kind of happened" stops feeling like an honest explanation and starts sounding like an alarm. You realize much of your life has been organized around other people's needs, expectations, and timing, while your own choices trail behind like an afterthought.

You still wake up, work, show up, and get things done. Nothing is falling apart. But a quiet truth surfaces you are being carried more by momentum than by intention.

◆ The Landscape of Drift

Drift does not announce itself. It arrives disguised as normalcy.

You take the job because it was offered, not because you wanted it. You stay in a relationship because leaving feels harder than staying, not because staying feels good. You agree with the plans because everyone else seems excited, not because you actually want to go. You say yes because no one else will do it, not because you have capacity.

At first, these feel like reasonable compromises. Life is complicated. You cannot always do exactly what you want. Being an adult means being flexible, accommodating, willing to put your own preferences aside sometimes.

But somewhere along the way, "sometimes" became "almost always." And flexibility became erasure.

Drift is what happens when you stop asking yourself what you actually want and start defaulting to what seems easiest, safest, or least likely to disappoint someone. It is the slow replacement of authorship with automation. Your days begin to feel like they are happening *to* you instead of being chosen *by* you.

The strange part is that drift can look very successful from the outside. You might have a good job, a stable relationship, a full calendar. People might describe you as responsible, reliable, grounded. You are not failing. You are functioning.

But functioning is not the same as living. And somewhere inside, you know it.

◆ What Drift Looks Like in Different Contexts

In work:

You stay in a job that stopped challenging you years ago because it pays well and leaving feels risky. You take on projects you do not care about because someone asked and you did not want to seem difficult. You attend meetings where your input is not valued but you show up anyway because "that's just how it is." You spend your days reacting to emails, putting out fires, managing other people's urgency, and by the time you get home, you realize you have made almost no choices of your own all day.

In relationships:

You agree to plans you do not want because saying no feels selfish. You listen to the same complaints from the same friend, offering the same advice that is never taken, and you do not ask yourself why you keep showing up for a dynamic that drains you. You stay in a partnership that is fine but not fulfilling because leaving would hurt someone and you do not want to be the person who causes pain. You let your family dictate how you spend holidays, how you raise your children, what decisions are acceptable—and you tell yourself it is just easier this way.

In parenting:

You say yes to every school event, every carpool request, every last-minute favor because "good parents show up." You organize your entire life around your children's needs and tell yourself that is what love looks like, even though you cannot remember the last time you did something just for yourself. You drift through the days in service to everyone else's schedule, and by the time your children are grown, you realize you forgot to have a life of your own.

In creative or personal life:

You used to write, paint, play music, or build things. But life got busy, and you put those things aside "for now." Years later, you still say you will get back to them "when things calm down," but things never calm down because you keep saying yes to everything else. You admire people who make time for their passions and tell yourself they must have more discipline, more time, better circumstances—when the truth is simpler: they decided, and you drifted.

◆ The Resistance You Will Feel

When you first begin to notice you are drifting, the resistance is immediate and loud.

The voice of guilt says:

"If you start saying no, people will think you are selfish. You will let them down. They need you. Who are you to prioritize your own wants over their needs?"

The voice of fear says:

"If you actually choose, you might choose wrong. What if you regret it? What if you disappoint someone important? What if being honest about what you want costs you a relationship, a job, a sense of safety?"

The voice of exhaustion says:

"I do not even know what I want anymore. It is easier to just keep doing what I am doing. At least this way, I do not have to think about it."

All of these voices are understandable. They are trying to protect you from discomfort, from conflict, from the vulnerability of claiming your own life.

But here is what they do not tell you: drift has a cost too.

The cost is a life that feels less and less like yours. The cost is resentment that builds quietly underneath—not toward the people making demands of you, but toward yourself for never saying no. The cost is the slow erosion of your sense of agency, until you genuinely believe you have no choice, even in moments where you clearly do.

The resistance is real. But so is the cost of staying in drift.

◆ The Moment the Threshold Becomes Visible

For most people, the threshold does not announce itself with clarity. It arrives as a feeling—vague, uncomfortable, difficult to name.

You might be sitting in traffic on your way to a job you do not care about and feel a wave of something close to grief. You might be agreeing to plans and feel your chest tightened, even though you cannot explain why. You might be lying in bed at night, reviewing your day, and realize you have made almost no decisions that felt like they came from you.

The threshold becomes visible the moment you stop explaining the feeling away and start paying attention to it.

That uncomfortable tightness? That is your body telling you that you just said yes while meaning no. That vague grief? That is the part of you that knows you are drifting and wants you to stop.

That sense of numbness? That is what happens when you have been on autopilot so long you forgot what it feels like to actually choose.

You do not cross this threshold by having a plan or by making one perfect decision. You cross it by admitting, with as much honesty as you can manage: "I have been drifting. And I do not want to drift anymore."

That admission is enough. It does not solve anything immediately. But it changes something fundamental: you can no longer pretend that your life is just happening to you. You know, now, that you are choosing—even when your choice is to not choose.

And once you know that you cannot unknow it.

📖 ✧ Tale vignette - The End of "It Just Happened."

A man rides the same train, works the same job, keeps the same schedule. One morning, a minor delay traps him between stations with no signal on his phone. In the unplanned stillness, he finally hears a thought he has been outrunning for years: "If nothing interrupts this, next year will look exactly the same."

The train moves again. His day continues. But something in him no longer accepts "it just happened" as a full story.

◆ Questions to Carry with You

These are not questions to answer once and move on. They are questions to hold lightly in the back of your mind as you move through your days. Let them surface when they need to.

Where in your life do you describe things as "just how it is" instead of as choices you are making or allowing?

Notice the language you use. Do you say, "I have to" when you mean "I am choosing to because the alternative feels worse"?

How often do you feel more carried by than choosing—in work, in relationships, in the way you spend your time?

Pay attention to moments when you feel like a passenger in your own life. What does that feel like in your body?

If your life paused "between stations" for ten quiet minutes, what truth might finally catch up to you?

What thought have you been outrunning? What admission are you avoiding?

What would need to change for you to feel like you are living your life instead of managing it?

Not everything needs to change. But what is one small thing—that would make your days feel more like they are yours?

What are you afraid would happen if you stopped drifting and started deciding?

Name the fear. Do not dismiss it. Understand it. And then ask: is that fear more costly than staying where you are?

Threshold 2 – Seeing Where
You Quietly Disappear

Disappearing is being physically there but emotionally gone—watching your life from the edges instead of feeling like you are actually in it.

You start to notice there are rooms where you do not fully arrive. You are present but edited. You play the helpful one, the steady one, the entertaining one, the agreeable one—but afterward, you feel strangely absent from your own memories of what just happened.

This threshold is crossed the moment you admit: "I am here, but not really here. They see what I do; they do not see me."

◆ The Landscape of Disappearance

Disappearance is different from drifting. Drifting is about your choices. Disappearance is about your presence.

You can drift through your life and still be fully there for certain moments—with a close friend, in creative flow, in moments of genuine intimacy. But disappearance is something else. It is being physically present while being emotionally or authentically absent.

It happens quietly. You walk into a room and before you even sit down, you are already managing the atmosphere. You notice the person who looks tired and you adjust your energy to comfort them. You hear the tension in the conversation, and you reach for a joke to lighten it. You sense the need and you fill it. You become useful immediately, and by becoming useful, you become invisible.

The strange thing is that people often respond to this version of you. They relax. They feel better. They tell you you are a good friend, a good family member, a good colleague. And because they are responding positively, you believe you are doing the right thing. It does not feel like disappearing. It feels like showing up.

But there is a cost.

The cost is that no one is actually meeting you. They are meeting the version of you that exists to make them comfortable. And over time, you stop being able to tell the difference between the version you are showing them and the version that is actually you.

Disappearance happens because, at some point, you learned that your full self was too much. Your emotions were too big, your needs were too demanding, your authenticity was inconvenient. So, you learned to compress yourself. You learned to be the person who listens instead of the person who is heard. The person who supports instead of the person who is supported. The person who manages instead of the person who is cared for.

This was intelligent. It kept you safe. It kept you connected. It kept you from being abandoned, rejected, or blamed for being difficult. But over time, the compression becomes so familiar that you forget you are compressing. You believe that this edited version is the only version you have to offer.

And you stop showing up fully—not because you are not there, but because you are not all there.

◆ What Disappearance Looks Like in Different Contexts

In close relationships:

You are the partner who always knows what the other person needs before they ask. You anticipate their moods, adjust your words, manage their emotions. You listen to their problems but rarely share your and when you do, you soften it, minimize it, apologize for taking up space. You leave conversations feeling more like a therapist than a lover. You realize, some-times in the middle of a moment you should be enjoying that you are not actually present. You are managing the interaction, making sure it goes smoothly, ensuring they feel good about you. And in that management, you are not there.

In friendships:

You are the one everyone calls when they need something. You show up, you help, you listen. But you notice that when you have a difficult time, people seem less available. And you do not ask them for help because you have become the helper. You have played this role for so long that it feels like truth. In rooms full of friends, you are entertaining them, reading them, keeping things light. Afterward, you realize no one asked how you were. And you wonder when that became okay.

In family:

You are the peacekeeper. The one who smooths over tensions, who makes everyone feel okay even when things are not okay. You hold the family's emotions. When your mother is anxious, you become calm, so she does not worry about you. When your sibling is struggling, you become strong, so they do not feel like they are burdening you. When your parents are angry, you become smaller, so they have space to express it. You have become so good at reading the room and adjusting yourself that you have forgotten what your own emotional baseline is.

In work:

You are the colleague who is always "on." You are dependable, pleasant, never a problem. You do not bring your full self to work—your doubts, your frustrations, your genuine opinions if they might rock the boat. You show up as the version of yourself that is easiest for everyone else. You are liked but not known. You are competent but disconnected from the work. You leave each day feeling like you performed in a play, and by Friday, you cannot remember a single authentic moment.

In social settings:

You are the person who makes conversation flow. You ask questions so others feel heard. You tell stories so the gathering does not feel awkward. You are charming, engaging, thoughtful. But driving home, you realize you did not share anything real. No one knows what you think or feel about anything that matters. You were present, but invisible. And you are not even sure why you showed up.

The Exhaustion of the Edit

Here is what people do not talk about when they talk about being a "good person" or a "good friend" or a "good family member": exhaustion.

The exhaustion of constantly monitoring yourself. Of listening to what is said and what is unsaid. Of managing multiple emotional realities, yours, and everyone else's. Of keeping your own needs in a drawer so you have space for someone else's. Of smiling when you are tired. Of being patient when you are frustrated. Of saying the kind thing instead of the true thing.

After years of this, you realize you are tired all the time. Not just physically tired, though that too. But tired in a way that rest does not fix. Tired because you are running two internal processes at once: the one where you experience reality, and the one where you manage how you appear in reality.

That dual consciousness is exhausting.

And because you have been doing it for so long, you have stopped noticing that you are doing it. It feels normal. It feels like just how you are.

But it is not. It is how you learned to survive in environments where your full presence was not safe.

◆ The Resistance You Will Feel

When you first notice you are disappearing, the resistance is immediate.

The voice of identity says:

"But this is who I am. I am the most helpful one. I am the person people can count on. If I stop being this, who am I? And if I am not this, will anyone still love me?"

The voice of responsibility says:

"People need me to show up this way. If I become honest about my feelings, authentic about my needs, real about my limits—I will hurt them. I will let them down. And I will be selfish."

The voice of fear says:

"If I show up fully, if I let people see the real me, they will reject it. They will leave. They will judge me. It is safer to be liked for what I do than to risk being hated for who I am."

The voice of habit says:

"I have been doing this for so long, I do not even know how to show up any other way. It feels impossible to be different."

All these voices are protecting you from something. But what they are protecting you from is the vulnerable act of being fully seen.

And what they do not tell you is that being fully seen is the only way real connection is possible.

◆ The Moment the Threshold Becomes Visible

For most people, the moment arrives quietly.

You might be in a conversation with someone you care about and notice, mid-sentence, that you are not actually saying what you feel. You are saying what you think they need to hear. And the gap between those two things suddenly becomes unbearable.

You might leave a gathering and realize that no one there knows what you really think about important things. And instead of feeling safe, you feel profoundly lonely.

You might catch yourself in a mirror, maybe in a moment of vulnerability, maybe just before you put your "game face" on—and not recognize the person looking back. And you realize that the recognition has been missing for so long you forgot what it felt like.

Or you might be sitting with someone you love and suddenly feel the distance between you, even though you are sitting close. And you understand: they do not know you. Not really. Because you have been too busy showing them who you thought they needed you to be.

The threshold is crossed when you finally admit: "I am here, but they are not meeting me. And I am not meeting myself."

That admission is painful. Because it means acknowledging that the strategy that has kept you safe and connected has also kept you alone—precisely because the person being met is not actually you.

But once you see it, you cannot unsee it.

📖 ✧ Tale vignette - When the Question Appeared

At a family dinner, a woman does what she always does: keeps conversation flowing, anticipates needs, softens tension with perfectly timed humor. Driving home in the dark, replaying the evening, she realizes she cannot recall a single moment when someone was actually curious about her.

The question that lands is simple and unsettling: "Did anyone see me tonight—or just what I do for them?"

◆ A Deeper Look: The Body's Refusal

There is something worth noting here: your body knows when you are disappearing, even if your mind does not want to admit it.

You might notice that you are tired after time with people you love. Not because the interaction was demanding, but because you were not fully there. You were managing. You were compressing. You were on.

You might notice that in certain relationships or certain rooms, you physically contract. Your chest tightens. Your voice gets smaller. You take up less space. Your body is telling you: "You are not safe to be fully here."

And sometimes your body refuses. You get anxious for no reason you can name. You feel depressed even though your life looks fine. You experience physical symptoms—tension, insomnia, and digestive issues that have no medical explanation. Your body is speaking a language your mind has learned to ignore: "This is costing you something."

Paying attention to the body's refusal is often the first step in noticing you are disappearing. Because the body does not lie. It does not perform. It does not manage. It simply knows you are not being authentic here. And it is responding to that knowledge.

◆ Questions to Carry with You

In which relationships or settings do you tend to shrink, perform, or stay on script?

Pay attention not just to what you do, but to how your body responds. Where does your chest tighten? Where do you take up less space?

Where do you leave gatherings feeling more useful than known?

Think about conversations where you did all the listening. Where you gave advice, no one asked for. Where you were helpful because it was safer than being vulnerable.

If you stopped managing the atmosphere, who would you be in the room?

Not as a permanent change—just for one moment, imagine showing up without the edit. What would be different?

What are you afraid that would happen if the people closest to you actually saw you—not the version of you that serves them, but the real you?

Name the fear. Do not rationalize it away. What is the catastrophe you are protecting them from?

Where in your life are you present but not there?

The distinction matters. Can you name a place where you show up physically but leave emotionally or authentically?

What would need to be true for you to show up more fully?

Not perfectly. Not without managing anything. Just a little more you, a little less edit.

Threshold 3 – Realizing Admiration Has Become Avoidance

Postponing is the quiet habit of putting off the changes you know you need, choosing short-term comfort over the long-term life you want.

You think you are just inspired by certain people—the calm friend, brave colleagues, creative strangers online. You study their routines, words, and choices the way someone studies a distant shore. It feels safe because you have quietly decided you are not that kind of person.

This threshold appears when you recognize: your admiration is not random. It is a mirror of something you have but have not yet chosen.

◆ The Landscape of Admiration as Avoidance

Admiration is one of the most socially acceptable forms of postponement.

When you admire someone, it feels virtuous. You are inspired. You are learning. You are motivated by their example. No one can criticize you for admiring someone. In fact, admiration is often praised as a sign of growth, of openness, of having good role models.

But there is a trap hidden inside admiration.

The trap is this: admiration can become a substitute for action.

You can spend years studying someone else's life, marveling at their choices, feeling inspired by their courage, and never once stepping into that same courage yourself. You can tell yourself that you are learning from them when what you are doing is using them as proof that you cannot be like that—not because you lack the capacity, but because they are different. They are braver, calmer, more creative, more disciplined. They are built differently than you.

And if you believe that, you never have to try.

Admiration becomes avoidance the moment it stops being inspiration and becomes an excuse. The moment you use someone else's example not to motivate yourself, but to explain why you cannot do what they do. The moment you study their life in such detail that you convince yourself you understand why they can do it and you cannot.

This is the subtle poison of admiration: it allows you to feel connected to the thing you want without risking anything to pursue it.

◆ What Admiration-as-Avoidance Looks Like in Different Contexts

In creativity:

You follow artists you admire obsessively. You study their process, read their interviews, watch their videos. You feel inspired every time you encounter their work. You tell people, "I want to create like that someday." But you do not create.

You study. And studying feels enough. You feel like you are doing something toward your goal because you are staying informed, staying inspired, staying connected to the idea of creating. But you are not creating. You are watching someone else create.

In career and ambition:

You admire people who took risks, left stable jobs, started businesses, pivoted themselves to new industries. You study how they did it. You listen to their podcasts. You read their books. You imagine yourself doing the same thing. But when it comes time to take the risk, you find reasons why your situation is different. You tell yourself that they have advantages you do not have, or more courage, or better circumstances. And you stay in the job you are unhappy with, telling yourself that you are still learning from their example.

In relationships and boundaries:

You have a friend or colleague who sets clear boundaries. They say no without explaining. They do not over-function in relationships. They seem so calm and at peace. You admire this so much. You study how they do it. You try to emulate them. But when you are in a situation where you need to set a boundary, you do not. You still say yes, still explain, still over-function. And you tell yourself that they are just naturally like that. That they do not have your responsibilities, your people, your complicated situations.

In health and wellness:

You follow people on social media who are fit, healthy, present. You admire their discipline. You study their routines. You buy the same supplements, try the same workouts, read the same books about nutrition. But you do not actually change how you live. You are gathering information about health without pursuing it. And the admiration feels like progress, even though nothing in your actual body has changed.

Fact: a large share of gym memberships go largely unused, and some people admit they like the feeling of being able to say they "belong to a gym" more than they like actually going.

In personal development:

You admire people who seem to have their lives figured out. They are present. They are honest. They set boundaries. They know what they want. You study them. You take notes on what they say. You try to understand how they became that way. But you are studying them instead of becoming. And the study feels safer than the becoming, because becoming requires risk and vulnerability.

◆ The Psychology of Borrowed Courage

Here is what happens psychologically when admiration becomes avoidance:

You place the quality you admire outside of yourself. You see it as something that belongs to them, that they possess, that makes them different from you. This externalizing feels protective. It means you do not have to question why you do not have it. It is not that you are choosing not to be brave, creative, or honest. It is just that you are not that kind of person.

But this belief is a trap.

Because the qualities you admire most in others are often qualities that already exist in you—just in an underdeveloped or unclaimed form. You recognize them in others precisely because some part of you knows them. The calm you admire exists in you, even if you have learned to override it with anxiety. The creativity you admire is in you, even if you have learned to prioritize practicality. The honesty you admire is in you, even if you have learned to soften it to avoid conflict.

You are not drawn to people who embody qualities you completely lack. You are drawn to people who embody qualities you have but have not yet claimed.

And that is a hugely different thing.

The Resistance You Will Feel

When you begin to recognize that your admiration might be avoidance, the resistance is immediate and compelling.

The voice of realism says:

"But they really are different from me. They have more talent, more confidence, more resources, more luck. It is not fair to compare myself to them."

The voice of protection says:

"If I admit that I could be like that, then I must try. And if I try and fail, that is worse than never trying."

The voice of safety says:

"Admiring from a distance is safe. Trying would be vulnerable. I could be rejected, judged, or fail publicly."

The voice of identity says:

"I am not that kind of person. That is who they are. I am someone different."

All these voices are protecting you from the vulnerability of claiming something you want. But what they do not tell you is that the distance you maintain through admiration comes with its own cost: the cost of never becoming.

The Moment the Threshold Becomes Visible

The moment usually arrives as a strange kind of discomfort.

You might be listening to someone you admire talk about their creative process, and instead of feeling inspired, you feel something closer to grief. Or envy. Or frustration. And you realize: *I have been listening to this person talk about their work for years, and I have not done my own work.*

Or you might catch yourself studying someone's life so intently that you realize you have become more informed about their choices than you are about your own. And you think: *Why do I know more about how they live than how I live?*

Or someone might ask you, "Why do you not just do that?" And you realize that all your careful, rational explanations for why you cannot do what they do sound thin. Sound like excuses. Sound like stories you have told yourself so many times that they have become invisible.

The threshold is crossed when you finally see it clearly: The person I admire is similar to me. They have simply chosen. And I have not.

That recognition is uncomfortable. Because it means you can no longer use their difference as proof of your limitation.

📖 ✧ Tale vignette – Part 1: When Admiration Turned Inward

A man listens to the same thoughtful podcast host every week, telling himself, "Some people are just built that way." One day the host says, in passing, "If you feel drawn to how someone lives, ask which part of you is asking to be claimed."

The sentence will not leave him. His admiration suddenly feels less like innocent inspiration and more like a responsibility he has been postponing.

📖 ✧ Tale vignette – Part 2: No Longer Just Watching

Later that week, the man meets a colleague who reminds him of the podcast host—calm, thoughtful, present in conversations. He finds himself studying this person, too, just as he studies the podcast. And then he stops himself.

He sits with an uncomfortable question: What if I am not trying to learn from them? What if I am using them as proof that I cannot be like that?

And for the first time, he considers: *What if I could be?*

◆ Questions to Carry with You

Who do you consistently admire, and what specific qualities—not achievements—draw you to them?

Think about the person, not their resume. What do they *do* that you find compelling?

What stories do you tell yourself about why you cannot live that way?

"They are just naturally like that." "They do not have my responsibilities." "I missed my chance." "I'm not built that way." Name the story. Say it aloud. How true is it, really?

If admiration is really recognition, what part of you is waiting to be owned?

Not someday. Not eventually. Right now, in some small form—where is this quality already alive in you?

Can you remember a time when you were the calm, brave, creative, honest person you admire in others?

Even if it was a long time ago. Even if it was small. Even if it was just for a moment. Can you find evidence that this quality is not foreign to you?

What would it look like to move from studying someone else's life to building your own in that direction?

Not becoming them. But become more fully yourself. What is one small step?

What are you afraid would happen if you stopped admiring and started trying?

Name the fear. Then ask: is that fear more costly than staying still?

◆ The Man in the Mirror Café

Michael Jackson's "Man in the Mirror" says the truth out loud: if something is going to change, it has to begin with the person standing in front of the mirror. Both his song and this tale are reaching toward the same place, but in different ways. They exist to bring you to that charged moment of recognition where it becomes undeniable that the life that must change is the one looking back at you.

This story moves more quietly. It does not arrive as an anthem, but as a single scene: one man, one café, a mirror that starts out as part of the décor and slowly becomes impossible to ignore. Where the song swells with a chorus, this tale works by subtle disturbance—a familiar room, a passing stranger, and a reflection that begins to look a little too much like the life he was meant to be living.

Their shared aim is the same: to move a person from distant wishing into personal responsibility. One does it with a rising hook you cannot get out of your head; the other with a quiet moment you cannot easily explain away. This is that quieter moment.

📖 Tale vignette - One – The Man in the Mirror Café

The Willow Café sat on the corner of Willow Street, easy to miss if you were walking fast and thinking about other things. The front window was usually a little fogged, even in summer, softening whatever was inside. A small brass bell over the door announced each customer with a gentle chime.

Daniel found it by accident one Tuesday when he turned left instead of right coming out of the station. He was running late and only ducked in because the usual coffee place had a line out the door. Inside, the air smelled like dark

roast and something faintly sweet, the kind of place that made time feel slower as soon as you stepped in.

He ordered a black coffee, no sugar, more than preference—and took the back booth, the one with the old mirror bolted to the wall. The glass was worn and clouded at the edges, not quite sharp enough to offer a clean reflection, more like a suggestion.

That first morning, he didn't notice anyone but his inbox.

He opened his laptop, burned his tongue on the first sip, and began answering emails he wouldn't remember sending. The bell chimed for other customers. Cups clinked, milk steamed, chairs scraped the floor. The café moved around him like a small, self-contained world he was technically in but not really part of.

The second morning, his feet turned left again.

He told himself it was just for the coffee. When he pushed open the door, the bell sounded its familiar chime. He slid into the same back booth, set his cup down, and let his eyes travel across the room.

That's when he saw him.

Across the aisle, in the opposite booth, sat a man in a crisp blue shirt. Sleeves neatly pressed. A thick book opened on the table, pages turning slowly, as if there were no particular rush to finish. He held his cup with both hands, elbows relaxed, shoulders easy. He looked like someone whose day had edges—clear, chosen—rather than someone constantly spilling into the next task.

Daniel watched the way people watch something they wish were true about themselves.

He told himself it was casual, just part of taking in the room. But his eyes kept returning to the steady figure in the blue shirt. A story formed quickly in his mind: a professor who wrote before sunrise, a consultant who didn't panic over email, a writer who actually finished the projects he started.

Whoever the man was, he seemed like a different category of person—one who moved from intention instead of from urgency.

Daniel's own mornings felt more like damage control: alarm snoozed three times, half-eaten breakfast, inbox already full, mind reacting to everything and choosing almost nothing. The man in the blue shirt became, in his imagination, the embodiment of all the ways he wasn't.

By the third morning, the café was no longer an accident. It was part of his route.

Same time. Same order. Same back booth with the mirror. And, almost always, the same man in the blue shirt across the aisle, already there, already settled. Daniel began to build small rituals around watching him. He pretended to check his phone while glancing up. He hovered over his keyboard a little longer, letting his gaze drift to the mirror.

In the clouded glass behind his own booth, he could see the man's reflection: softened at the edges, the blue of his shirt dulled by the aging silvering of the mirror. Somehow, the blur made the scene even more appealing, like a life viewed through a filter.

It felt oddly reassuring to believe the man was simply built differently. As long as he told himself that, Daniel didn't have to question anything about his own life. He could be inspired for twenty minutes and then go back to the familiar scramble.

One morning, the booth across the aisle was empty.

No blue shirt. No book. Just beige vinyl and a napkin dispenser he'd never paid attention to before.

Daniel checked his phone, though he wasn't expecting any particular message. He refreshed his inbox twice. He told himself the tightness in his chest was just caffeine on an empty stomach. Still, his eyes kept slipping back to the vacant seat with a kind of quiet urgency he didn't want to admit to.

Why does this bother me? he thought. I do not even know him.

The next day, the man was back.

Relief moved through Daniel so quickly it surprised him. He hid it behind an unnecessary sip of hot coffee. As he set the cup down, he caught the man's outline again in the mirror: the familiar blue, the stillness, the open book.

This time, Daniel let himself look a little longer.

The man shifted slightly, as if aware of being observed, and turned his head just enough that his eyes met Daniel's in the reflection. The contact was brief and softened by the cloudy glass, but unmistakable.

Daniel's chest tightened. It felt like being caught reading someone's private thoughts.

The man's mouth curved into a small, knowing smile. Not a flashy, everyone-in-the-room smile—just a quiet acknowledgment, like recognizing someone you have been aware of for a while.

"You come here to watch," he said.

His voice was calm, the words light, but they landed with more weight than their volume.

Daniel turned in his seat. Up close, the man looked more ordinary than the reflection had suggested: faint lines at the corners of his eyes, a small scar near his chin, a coffee ring on the table between them. Not a different species. Just a person.

"I—sorry," Daniel said. "I didn't mean to stare. I just—"

"You think I'm something you are not," the man said, gently interrupting.

There was no accusation in it. Just accuracy.

For a moment, the café sounds grew sharper: the hiss of the espresso machine, the clink of spoons, the low murmur of other conversations. Inside that small pocket of noise, Daniel searched for something to say. A dozen denials rose—Just daydreaming, just passing time—but none of them felt true enough to speak.

The man glanced at the mirror behind Daniel and tilted his head toward it.

"You do not admire me," he said. "You recognize me."

Then he stepped away from the booth, walked to the door, and left. The bell chimed once, briefly, and the door closed behind him.

Daniel sat very still.

He looked at the empty booth across the aisle: the seat, the tabletop, the napkin dispenser. Without the man, it looked completely unremarkable, as if it had never been special at all.

Slowly, he turned back to the mirror.

The glass reflected a man with a cooling coffee, a tired face, shoulders

held a little too high. Not as serene as the figure he'd been watching, but undeniably capable of softening. Capable of pausing. Capable of choosing something other than the familiar rush.

The calm he had admired in the man in the blue shirt was not a rare trait belonging to a rare kind of person. It was a way of moving through the world that had always been available to him—and that he had, up until now, kept at a safe distance by pretending it lived in someone else.

Believing the man was different had cost Daniel nothing. Owning the resemblance would cost him something: the story that his life could only ever be the way it was.

Sitting there in the back booth of the Mirror Café, Daniel realized that what he had been calling admiration was something more uncomfortable and more hopeful.

Recognition.

For the first time, he met his own eyes in the mirror on purpose.

And this time, he did not look away.

◆ Reflection After the Tale

After a story like *The Man in the Mirror Café*, reflection is less about dissecting the plot and more about noticing where it quietly overlaps with your own life.

Let these questions move slowly. They are invitations, not assignments.

1. Who is your "man in the blue shirt"?

   - Who do you find yourself watching or admiring from a distance, assuming they are made of something you are not?

   - In what parts of your life do you feel more like an observer of other people's lives than a participant on your own?

2. What, exactly, do you admire in them?

   - Is it their calm, their steadiness, their courage, their creativity, their freedom, their honesty?

   - If you had to reduce it to three words, which qualities are you truly drawn to—beneath the image or status?

3. Where do those qualities already exist in you—unused or under-used?

   - Can you remember even one moment when you were that calm, that brave, that honest, that present?

   - What made you decide that those moments "didn't count" or "weren't really you"?

4. How have you been watching your own life in reflection instead of inhabiting it directly?

   - Where do you spend more time imagining, planning, or comparing than actually stepping into the scene?

   - In which area of your life do you feel most like Daniel—sitting safely in the booth, watching a life you could, in some way, choose?

5. What story do you tell yourself about why you cannot live like the person you admire?

   - "They are just naturally like that." "They do not have my responsibilities." "I missed my chance."

   - If that story were not the final word, what small possibilities would quietly come back into view?

6. If admiration is actually recognition, what are you being asked to own?

   - Which part of you is this tale gently pointing to and saying, "This is yours too"?

   - What feels both uncomfortable and true when you admit, "I am not only inspired by that—I see myself in it"?

7. What is one small, concrete choice that would feel like turning toward the mirror?

   - Not a total reinvention—just one choice this week that moves you slightly from watching to participating.

   - How might your day feel different if you treated that small choice as evidence that the life you admire is not separate from you?

You do not need to answer all of these, now or ever. Often, the question you resist the most is the one standing closest to your next inner threshold.

◆ A Deeper Look: Recognition Versus Inspiration

There is a distinction worth making here between genuine inspiration and admiration-as-avoidance.

Genuine inspiration moves you toward action. It says: "I see someone doing something I value, and it makes me want to try." It is generative. It creates energy and momentum.

Admiration-as-avoidance keeps you still. It says: "I see someone doing something I value, and it proves I cannot do it." It is static. It consumes energy without generating anything.

The difference is subtle but crucial. And you can feel the difference in your body. Genuine inspiration makes you want to move. Admiration-as-avoidance makes you want to study, to analyze, to understand—but not to do.

Pay attention to which one you are experiencing.

Threshold 4 – Meeting the Part of You That Kept Waiting for "Later"

Performing is playing the role that's expected of you instead of telling the truth—managing your image so well that you start to lose sight of yourself.

"Later" can become a very crowded place. You put ideas, desires, and versions of yourself there: when things calm down, when the kids are older, when you make more money, when you feel more confident.

This threshold is crossed when you see that "later" has quietly turned into "never," and that the self you kept postponing has been waiting in the doorway the whole time.

◆ The Landscape of Postponement

Postponement is different from patience. Patience is a choice you make with awareness. Postponement is a choice you make and then forget you made it.

You put something away temporarily. You tell yourself it is just for now. Just until this crisis passes. Just until you get through this season. Just until you have more time, more money, more clarity, more confidence.

And then life does not calm down. Another crisis arrives. The season you thought was temporary becomes permanent. The "someday" you kept promising yourself never comes on its own. It requires a decision. And decisions are hard.

So instead of deciding, you keep postponing. And the things you put in the "later" drawer, the dreams, the projects, the versions of yourself you meant to become—they wait. They do not leave. They do not go bad. They just wait, patiently, for you to come back.

The tragic part is that you forget they are waiting.

You forget that you once wanted to write, paint, or learn, or travel, or have a conversation you have been avoiding, or risk something that matters to you. You push the thought down so many times that eventually, it stops surfacing. And you tell yourself: *I guess I did not want that after all.*

But you did. And you do. You just learned to live without it.

Postponement works because it is disguised as responsibility. You are not selfish by putting your dreams on hold. You are mature. You are a good parent, a good partner, a good employee. You are doing what needs to be done. And when people tell you that you are selfless, responsible, and strong, you feel good about the choice to postpone. You feel like you are doing the right thing.

What postponement does not tell you is that postponing yourself has a cost too.

The cost is a slow erosion of hope. The cost is the things you never do because you kept waiting for the right time. The cost is the person you meant to become but never did. The cost is the ache that shows up sometimes—in the middle of an ordinary day—where you suddenly feel grief for a life you never lived.

◆ What Postponement Looks Like in Different Contexts

In creativity:

You used to write, or paint, or make music, or build things. But life got busy. School, work, family, obligations. And you thought: *I will come back to this when things calm down.* Years passed. Decades, sometimes. And you never came back. Now you tell yourself that you are too old, too out of practice, too tired. But the truth is simpler: you postponed so long that you forgot you were allowed to want it.

In career:

You took the job that was offered because you needed the money, it was practical, or it was what was expected. You told yourself it was temporary—just a few years until you figured out what you wanted to do. But the job became comfortable. It paid the bills. People knew you there. And the thought of changing, of risking, of trying something you cared about, that thought got smaller until it disappeared. Now you tell yourself you are too old to change, too trapped by responsibility. But you have simply postponed the choice for so long that choosing feels impossible.

In relationships:

There is a conversation you need to have. A boundary you need to set. A truth you need to tell. But you keep waiting for the right time. When they are less stressed. When you have figured out how to say it right. When the risk feels smaller. But the right time never comes. And the conversation awaits. And you wait. And the relationship slowly erodes from the thing left unsaid.

In education or skill-building:

You always meant to learn something. Go back to school. Learn a language. take a class in something that interests you. But you kept postponing. And now you tell yourself: *I am too old. I missed my window.* But you have simply made a different choice to not try rather than the choice to try and fail.

In health and self-care:

You know you should move your body, rest, eat differently, go to therapy, address the thing that has been bothering you. But you keep telling yourself: *Later when I have time. Later, when things calm down. Later, when I have more energy.* And later never comes. And your health slowly erodes because you kept postponing the care you knew you needed.

◆ The Grief of Recognition

One of the strangest parts of crossing this threshold is the grief that comes with it.

You realize that years have passed. Opportunities have closed. You are not the age you were when you first put the dream away. Some of the people you meant to talk to are gone. Some of the doors you meant to walk through have closed.

And you must grieve that. You must grieve the version of yourself you meant to become but did not. You must grieve the time you spent waiting for "later" instead of living now.

This grief is not weakness. It is honesty. And it is essential.

Because you cannot move forward until you acknowledge what the postponement cost you.

◆ The Resistance You Will Feel

When you notice that "later" has become "never," the resistance is both quiet and enormous.

The voice of regret says:

"It is too late now. I waited too long. I should have done it when I had the chance."

The voice of fear says:

"If I start now, I will fail. I will be bad at it. I will regret trying."

The voice of responsibility says:

"I cannot do this now. People still need me. I still must manage everything. How can I prioritize my own wants?"

The voice of protection says:

"It is safer to not want anything. Then I cannot be disappointed."

All these voices are protecting you from the vulnerability of wanting something, trying something, risking something.

But what they do not tell you is that the cost of not trying is higher than the cost of trying and failing.

◆ The Moment the Threshold Becomes Visible

The moment often arrives unexpectedly.

You might be cleaning out a closet and find a notebook full of ideas you once had. Or you might overhear someone your age doing the thing you always meant to do and feel a sharp pang of something close to envy. Or you might look in the mirror and think: *How much longer am I going to wait?*

Or it might be quieter. You might be lying in bed at night and realize that you have been saying "later" for so long that you have forgotten what it was you meant to do later.

The threshold is crossed when you finally see it clearly: "Later" has not protected me. It has only delayed me. And I am running out of time to not wait anymore.

That recognition is both terrifying and oddly liberating.

Because once you see it, you have a choice you did not have before. You can keep waiting. Or you can begin—not someday, but now, in whatever small way is available to you now.

📖 ✧ Tale vignette - When Someday Didn't Arrive

On a random afternoon, a woman, opening an old box while cleaning a closet, finds a notebook full of songs she wrote in her twenties. In the

JORGE ARMENTEROS

margins are phrases like "When life settles" and "Someday I'll record these." Decades later, she realizes life never sent an official notice that "someday" had arrived; it just kept walking.

She suddenly sees that survival has stopped being a season and has become her entire way of being.

◆ A Deeper Look: The Cost of Deferred Living

There is research that shows that people who postpone meaningful goals experience higher rates of depression, lower life satisfaction, and a sense of disconnection from their own lives. This is not because postponement is sometimes bad. It is because constantly deferring what matters to you erodes your sense of agency and hope.

When you tell yourself "later" enough times, you stop believing in the possibility of change. You stop trusting yourself to make your own decisions. You become increasingly identified with the role you are playing in other people's lives, and increasingly invisible to yourself.

The self you are postponing does not disappear. But it does become quieter. And the longer it waits, the harder it is to hear.

◆ Questions to Carry with You

What dreams, projects, or parts of yourself have you repeatedly filed under "later"?

Do not judge. Just notice. What is waiting?

How long have some of those "latter's been waiting?

Be honest with yourself about how long you have been saying "later" for the same thing.

If "later" never becomes less complicated than now, what tiny step could you take toward one of them anyway?

Not a big step. Just one small step that says: "This matters to me, and I am going to begin."

What are you afraid would happen if you stopped waiting and started doing?

That you would fail? That you would succeed and must commit to it? That you would disappoint someone.

When you imagine yourself at the end of your life looking back, what would you regret more: trying and failing, or never trying at all?

Sit with that question. Do not answer it quickly.

What is one small way you could resurrect one postponed part of yourself this week?

Not as a solution. Just as a way of saying: "I see you. You have waited long enough."

Threshold 5 – Feeling the Cost of Performing Instead of Living

There is a point where being impressive stops feeling satisfying and starts feeling exhausting. You realize that much of your energy goes into looking okay, sounding okay, and making sure everyone else is okay with you—even when you are not okay.

This threshold arises when the performance no longer pays the emotional bills you thought it did.

◆ The Landscape of Performance

Performance is not dishonesty, exactly. It is a kind of selective truth-telling.

You are being honest—but you are selecting which truths to tell and which to hide. You are being yourself—but a carefully edited version of yourself. You are showing up—but you are showing up as the person you think you are supposed to be, not the person you are.

Performance starts early. In childhood, you learn that certain parts of you are acceptable and certain parts are not. You learn which emotions earn approval and which create distance. You learn which version of you makes people feel comfortable and which makes them uncomfortable.

So, you begin to perform that comfortable version. And you do it so well, and for so long, that you eventually believe it is the only version you have.

The problem with performance is that it works. At least at first.

People respond positively to the version of you that you are performing. They like you. They trust you. They lean on you. They feel comfortable around you. And because they are responding well, you believe you are doing the right thing. You believe the performance is who you are.

But somewhere along the way, something shifts.

The performance that once felt like strategy starts to feel like a prison. The mask that once protected you starts to suffocate you. The version of you that everyone likes starts to feel like a lie. And you realize: people are responding well to someone I am not.

And the emptiness of that realization is devastating.

◆ What Performance Looks Like in Different Contexts

At work:

You are the colleague who is always "on." You arrive with energy, even when you are exhausted. You manage problems without showing stress. You keep things light and positive even when you are struggling. You never bring your full self to work—your doubts, your frustrations, your genuine opinions if they might rock the boat. You have become so good at performing competence that people do not know you are drowning. And you keep performing because the moment you stop, you fear people will see that you are not as capable as they think.

In relationships:

You are the partner who has it together. You do not bring your insecurities, your fears, your needs. You show up as the strong one, the capable one, the one who does not need support. Your partner does not know you are struggling because you have not let them see you struggle. You perform contentment even when you are unhappy. You perform satisfaction even when you are resentful. And over time, they feel like they know you—but they only know the performance.

In friendship:

You are the entertaining friend. You make people laugh. You remember their birthdays. You are the one people can count on. But you never let them see you struggling. You never ask for help. You perform fine so consistently that when you are not fine, no one notices. And the loneliness of that—of being liked for the performance while the real you go unseen—is profound.

In family:

You are the successful one, the responsible one, the one who has their life figured out. So, you perform that, even when you do not have it figured out. Your family believes in your competence, so you maintain the performance because disappointing them feels unbearable. You never let them see your failures or your struggles. And they love you—but they love the performance.

On social media:

You create a version of your life that looks good, feels aspirational, makes people admire you. You show the highlight reels and hide the behind-the-scenes. You perform a life you think people want to see. And thousands of people "like" this performance. And you feel alone.

In creative work:

You are the artist, the writer, the creator who always has something finished, polished, impressive to show. So, you perform competence. You do not show the messy first drafts, the failed experiments, the pieces you are uncertain about. You only show the work that is already perfect. And as a result, you rarely try anything new, because trying new things means risking being seen as not competent.

◆ The Exhaustion of the Mask

Performance is exhausting in a way that is hard to explain to someone who has not done it.

It is not the exhaustion of hard work. It is the exhaustion of constant vigilance. Of monitoring yourself. Of adjusting in real-time based on how the other person is responding. Of holding a story about who you are supposed to be while simultaneously trying to live as that person.

Your nervous system never fully relaxes. Some part of you is always on. Some part of you is always calculating: Is this the right thing to say? Is this the right way to say it? Are they buying it? Do they suspect that I am not actually like this?

After years of this, you realize you are tired all the time. Not just physically tired, though that too. But tired in a way that disconnects you from your own life.

Because performance requires that you be outside of your own experience. You must observe yourself. You must manage yourself. You must be the audience to your own performance.

And when you are the audience to your own performance, you are not actually present in your own life. You are slightly outside of it, watching, managing, adjusting.

The loneliness of that is enormous.

◆ The Resistance You Will Feel

When you first notice that the performance is exhausting you, the resistance is powerful.

Your identity says:

"But this is who I am. I am the competent one, the strong one, the one who has it together. If I stop performing this, who am I?"

Your fear says:

"If people see the real me—my doubts, my struggles, my imperfections—they will leave. They will judge me. They will abandon me."

Your responsibility says:

"People depend on me being this way. If I show them, I am struggling, I will let them down."

Your shame says:

"The real me is not good enough. The performance is the only acceptable version."

All these voices are protecting you from the vulnerability of being authentically seen. But what they do not tell you is that the performance itself is a form of abandonment—of yourself.

◆ The Moment the Threshold Becomes Visible

The moment often arrives as a sudden rupture in the facade.

You might be in a meeting, performing competence, and catch your reflection in a window and not recognize yourself. Or you might be at a social gathering, entertaining people, and suddenly feel so distant from yourself that you cannot remember what you think about anything.

Or someone might say to you, "You always have it together," and instead of feeling complimented, you feel devastated. Because you realize: they do not know me. And I have spent years making sure they do not know me.

Or you might be alone, finally, and realize that you have no idea what you actually want, what you actually think, what you actually feel—because you have been so focused on what you think you should want, think, and feel.

The threshold is crossed when you finally admit I am exhausted from being who everyone thinks I am. And no one knows who I am.

That recognition is both relieving and terrifying. Because it means you have a choice: you can keep performing and keep being exhausted and unseen. Or you can begin, very carefully and very slowly, to let people see you.

📖 ✧ Tale vignette – Part One: Caught Out of Character

A man known at work for always being "on"—joking, upbeat, unbothered—catches his reflection in a restroom mirror after a meeting and does not recognize the tired eyes looking back. Without the smile and the commentary, his face looks hollow.

He realizes he does not actually know how to walk into a room without entertaining everyone. The thought, "What if I didn't have to?" feels terrifying and oddly relieving at the same time.

📖 ✧ Tale vignette – Part Two: The Face Without the Smile

That evening, at home alone, he tries something. He sits without distraction. He does not scroll, does not watch anything, does not fill the silence. He just sits and notices: he does not know what he wants. He does not know what he thinks about things that matter. He knows how to perform opinions, but he does not know his actual opinions.

And he understands something he has been avoiding: the performance has not protected him. It has hidden him. And he is lonely inside it.

◆ A Deeper Look: The Cost of Being Liked for Your Mask

Research in psychology shows that people who consistently perform rather than be authentic experience higher rates of depression, anxiety, and a persistent sense of disconnection. They may be socially successful—liked, admired, praised—but they experience their success as hollow because it is not based on their real self.

The cruel irony is this: the people who like you for your performance do not actually like you. They like the version you are showing them. And you know that. Which means you can never fully trust their affection.

Real connection requires real vulnerability. And as long as you are performing, you are not vulnerable. You are protected. And protected people cannot be truly seen.

◆ Questions to Carry with You

Where do you feel obligated to be "on," even when you are depleted?

Notice the spaces where you cannot be tired, cannot struggle, cannot be fully human.

What are you afraid would happen if you stopped performing and told the truth?

Not all the truth. Just some of it. What is the catastrophe you are protecting against?

How much of your life is spent maintaining an image instead of inhabiting yourself?

Think about your day. How much of your energy goes to managing how you appear?

Can you remember a time when you felt truly seen by someone—when you did not have to perform?

What was different? What did that feel like?

What would it look like to be liked for who you are, rather than who you perform?

What would you have to risk finding out?

What is one small way you could be slightly more authentic this week?

Not a total transformation. Just one small crack in the facade. What would that be?

Threshold 6 – Recognizing Survival Has Replaced Living

Surviving is getting through the day with no energy left for anything beyond that—living in constant overload, where there is no room to ask what you really want.

You have become very good at getting through things. You can manage schedules, handle crises, absorb stress, and carry more than anyone realizes. For a while, this feels like strength.

Then a quiet realization arrives you are not just going through a survival season—you have built your identity around surviving.

◆ The Landscape of Survival Mode

Survival mode is an intelligent response to crisis. When something dangerous or demanding arrives, your system activates. You focus on what is essential. You become efficient. You do what needs to be done. Your body releases adrenaline, your mind narrows, your emotions compress. You are built to survive.

The problem is when survival becomes permanent.

When the crisis passes, but you do not shift out of crisis mode. When the emergency ends, but your nervous system stays activated. When the threat is gone, but you keep moving like there is still a threat.

This happens to people who have experienced real loss, real danger, and sustained hardship. It also happens to people who have simply lived with chronic low-level stress, the kind that comes from being responsible for too much, being needed by too many people, never having permission to rest.

Over time, survival mode starts to feel like the only way you know how to be.

You become the person who can handle anything. Who never falls apart. Who always knows what to do? People lean on you because they can feel your steadiness. And you lean into being the steady one because it gives your life shape, a purpose, a reason to wake up.

But underneath the steadiness is exhaustion. Underneath the capability is numbness. Underneath competence is a kind of despair—because you realize that you are exceptionally good at surviving, but you have forgotten how to live.

◆ The Difference Between Surviving and Living

This distinction is important because many people confuse them.

Surviving is about doing. About getting through. About managing what needs to be managed so that you can exist another day.

Living is about being. About presence. About joy, curiosity, rest, play, connection, meaning things that are not "necessary" in the survival sense, but are necessary in the human sense.

When you are in survival mode, these things disappear. Not because you do not want them, but because they feel like luxuries you cannot afford. You are too busy handling the essentials to have space for the things that make life worth living.

In survival mode, you:

Wake up and move straight into action.

Do not pause to notice how you feel.

Check off tasks instead of experiencing moments.

Respond to urgency from other people instead of tending to your own needs.

Fall asleep exhausted and wake up the same way.

Cannot remember the last time you did something just for pleasure.

Have forgotten what you enjoy, what brings you joy, what makes you feel alive.

In living mode, you:

Create space for rest, even amid responsibility.

Notice how you feel and what you need.

Experience moments, not just manage them.

Make time for what matters to you, even if it is not urgent.

Move through your day with some sense of choice about how you spend your energy.

Remember what brings you joy and make space for it.

Feel present in your own life.

The gap between these two states is enormous. And most people in survival mode do not realize how wide the gap has become.

◆ What Survival Mode Looks Like in Different Contexts

In parenting:

You wake up. Kids need breakfast, lunch packed, permission slips signed, rides to activities, homework checked, dinner made, bedtime managed. Your own needs—for rest, for adult conversation, for time to yourself—feel like selfish luxuries. You are in constant motion. By the end of the day, you are depleted. You love your children. But you do not remember what it feels like to enjoy them. You are too busy managing them.

In caregiving:

You are caring for an aging parent, a sick partner, a child with special needs. Your schedule is organized entirely around their needs. Your identity has fused with being the caregiver. You have become so good at handling crises that you do not know how to do anything else. You have forgotten what you enjoy, what you want, what matters to you. Rest feels like abandonment.

In work:

You took on more responsibility because the company needed it, or because you feared what would happen if you did not. Now you are essential, indispensable. Your job expands to fill every hour. You check emails at night. You think about work problems when you are trying to rest. You cannot take time off because everything falls apart without you. You are surviving your job, not doing your job.

In chronic stress:

You have lived with financial instability, housing insecurity, health challenges, or other ongoing difficulties for so long that you have forgotten what safety feels like. Your body is always a little bit on alert. Your mind is always a little bit planning for the next thing that could go wrong. You move through life in a kind of sustained tension. Rest is impossible because the thing you are worried about is still real.

◆ The Cost of Permanent Survival Mode

The body is not designed to be in survival mode indefinitely.

When you live in sustained activation—when your nervous system never fully relaxes, when your mind never fully disengages, when you never give yourself permission to truly rest—something breaks. Not dramatically, usually. But slowly.

You might notice:

A chronic tiredness that sleep does not fix.

Anxiety that has no specific source

Difficulty concentrating or thinking clearly.

Aches and pains without medical explanation

Emotional numbness or flatness

Difficulty feeling joy even when good things happen.

A sense of disconnection from your own life

Irritability or anger that seems disproportionate.

Loss of interest in things you used to enjoy.

These are not signs of weakness. They are signs that your system has been running on crisis mode for too long.

And here is what survival mode will never tell you: the crisis does not actually require you to be in crisis mode anymore. The threat has passed. Your system can relax. But you must give it permission.

◆ The Resistance You Will Feel

When you notice that survival mode has become your default, the resistance is both internal and external.

Your body says:

"But if I relax, if I stop being vigilant, something will go wrong. I am the only thing holding this together."

Your identity says:

"I am the person who can handle anything. If I am not handling everything, who am I?"

The people around you say:

"You are so strong. You always figure it out. We need you to keep doing this."

Your own mind says:

"Rest is lazy. Rest is irresponsible. Rest means giving up."

All these voices are protecting you from something. But what they are protecting you from is the vulnerability of being human needing rest, needing help, needing to take care of yourself.

And what they do not tell you is that you cannot help anyone else if you are running on empty. That strength without rest becomes fragile. That the most responsible thing you can do is take care of yourself.

◆ The Moment the Threshold Becomes Visible

For many people, the moment arrives as a question.

Someone asks: "How are you, really?" And you realize you do not know. You have been so busy handling everything that you have lost touch with how you are.

Or you have a moment where you realize: *I cannot keep doing this.* Not someday. But right now. Your body is telling you. Your mind is asking. Your spirit is whispering: *There must be more to life than this.*

Or you notice that you are no longer enjoying the things you are doing. You are just doing them. And the doing has become so automatized that you might as well be a robot.

The threshold is crossed when you finally admit: "I am surviving. But I am not living. And I do not remember what living feels like anymore."

That admission is often the beginning of everything changing.

Because once you see that survival has replaced living, you have a choice. You can keep surviving. Or you can begin, even in small ways, to live again.

📖 ✧ Tale vignette - When There Was No Space for Her

A caregiver opens her calendar and sees every square filled with other people's appointments: children, clients, parents, commitments. Her own name is nowhere. When someone casually asks what she does "just for herself," the question lands like a language she used to speak and has forgotten.

She suddenly sees that survival has stopped being a season and has become her entire way of being.

◆ A Deeper Look: The Body's Exhaustion

Your body keeps score. When you live in survival mode, your nervous system is constantly activated—the part of your brain that handles threats is always partially online. Your immune system is compromised because your body is prioritizing immediate survival over long-term health. Your sleep is lighter because part of you is always alert. Your digestion is off. Your sex drive diminishes. Your pain tolerance decreases even as your pain increases.

The body is designed to survive crisis for short periods. Days. Weeks. Not months. Not years. Not decades.

When you ask your body to stay in crisis mode indefinitely, it breaks in ways that are both visible and invisible. The visible ways are the symptoms. The invisible ways are the slow erosion of your will to be alive.

◆ Questions to Carry with You

In what ways has survival become your default, even when the crisis has technically passed?

Look at your calendar, your energy, your attention. What does survival mode look like in your daily life?

How do you justify never prioritizing your own restoration?

What story do you tell yourself about why rest is not allowed, why care for yourself is selfish?

If survival were meant to be temporary, what would "living" look like, even in small, ordinary ways, now?

Not a vacation or a retreat. Just one small thing that is not about managing. What is it?

What are you afraid would happen if you stopped being the person who handles everything?

That things would fall apart? That people would see you are struggling. That you would disappoint someone.

When was the last time you did something purely for pleasure, with no purpose other than that it brought you joy?

Can you remember? Can you imagine doing it again?

What would need to be true for you to believe that taking care of yourself is not selfish?

What permission would you need to give yourself?

Threshold 7 – Hearing the Question That Will Not Go Away

The **Unshakable Question** is a question that refuses to disappear because it points toward a truth you are meant to face and a decision you can no longer avoid.

At certain points, a particular question begins to echo inside you. It might not be convenient, polite, or easy to answer—but it refuses to be silenced. You distract yourself, reason with yourself, and promise to deal with it later. It returns.

This threshold comes when you finally admit: "This question is not a phase. It is part of my truth."

◆ The Landscape of the Persistent Question

Questions are different from problems.

Problems can be solved. Questions can only be answered. And some questions sit with you for a long time before the answer becomes clear.

A persistent question is one that keeps surfacing, no matter how many times you push it down. It shows up in the shower. It wakes you at 3 a.m. It arrives during quiet moments when you are alone. It surfaces in conversations you are not even having. You are in the middle of the day and suddenly: *the question.*

And each time it arrives, you handle it the same way: you dismiss it.

It is not the right time to ask this.

This is just a phase.

This is selfish / ungrateful / dramatic.

I should not be thinking about this.

I will deal with it later.

And so, you push the question down. Back to wherever persistent questions live when you refuse to hear them.

But they do not go away. They wait. They returned. They knock on different doors. They show up in different forms.

And eventually, if you are paying attention, you realize this is not going away because it is not meant to go away. This is my truth trying to get my attention.

◆ What the Persistent Question Looks Like in Different Contexts

In career:

"Am I actually happy here, or just comfortable?" This question arrives every Sunday night. It shows up in the middle of a meeting you are leading. It surfaces when you see someone doing something you secretly want to do. And each time, you push it down. *Not the right time. I have responsibilities. I should be grateful if I have a job.* But the question keeps coming back. Because part of you know the answer, even if you are not ready to admit it.

In relationships:

"Do I love this person or am I just afraid to be alone?"

This question arrives in the quiet moments. When you are lying in bed next to someone you care about but do not feel connected to. When you imagine a life without them and feel relief instead of devastation. And you push it down. *This is just a rough patch. Everyone feels this sometimes. I should not be thinking about this.* But the question persists. Because your body knows something your mind is not ready to accept.

In identity:

"Whose life am I actually living?"

This question can arrive in many forms. Is this the life I chose, or the life I was told to choose? Am I being myself, or am I being what everyone expects? Am I doing what I want, or what I think I should want? And the question is so unsettling that you immediately find ways to avoid it. I am being dramatic. This is ungrateful. Everyone feels this sometimes. But it keeps coming back because at some level, you know the answer is important.

In purpose:

"What am I doing this for?"

You are successful. You are accomplished. You have achieved things you thought would make you happy. And yet—*why does this not feel like enough?* The question feels almost insulting, as if you should be grateful and stop asking. But the question persists because achievement is not the same as meaning.

In authenticity:

"Am I being honest or performing?"

This question can show up anywhere—in relationships, at work, in social settings. You are in the middle of something and suddenly you notice *I am not actually myself right now. I am being who I think I should be.* And the question is uncomfortable because it means admitting that much of what you are doing is performed rather than authentic.

✦ The Discomfort of Taking the Question Seriously

There is a reason we dismiss persistent questions. Because taking them seriously requires something: engagement.

If you ignore the question, you can stay the same. You can keep living the life you are living, making the choices you are making, being the person, you have been.

But if you take the question seriously, if you sit with it, if you allow yourself to consider the possible answers, if you admit that the answer might require change—then you cannot stay the same.

And change is terrifying.

So instead, we minimize the question. We call it drama. We call it a midlife crisis. We call it ungrateful, selfish, immature. We find every reason to dismiss it.

But the question does not go away because it is not really a question. It is a truth trying to surface. It is your inner self trying to get your attention. It is the part of you that knows you are living something that is not aligned with who you are.

And that part does not give up. It keeps knocking. It keeps asking. It keeps returning until you finally pay attention.

◆ The Resistance You Will Feel

When you begin to take a persistent question seriously, the resistance is immediate and multifaceted.

Your identity resists:

"If I ask this question seriously, I might have to change. And I do not want to change. I am comfortable with who I am."

Your loyalty resists:

"If I ask this question, I might discover that the life I have built, the choices I have made, were not the right ones. And that feels like a betrayal of the people who are counting on me."

Your fear resists:

"If I answer this question honestly, I might have to do something difficult. Something that will upset people. Something that will make things complicated."

Your shame resists:

"I should not be asking this question. Good people do not ask this. Grateful people do not ask this. I am bad / ungrateful / selfish for even wondering."

All these resistances are protecting you from the vulnerability of change. But what they do not tell you is that ignoring the question has a cost too: the cost of living a life that is not yours.

◆ The Moment the Threshold Becomes Visible

The moment usually arrives as a kind of surrender.

You might be in conversation with someone, and they ask the question you have been avoiding, and instead of deflecting, you find yourself answering honestly. Or you might be alone and simply tired of pushing the question down, and you let yourself sit with it for the first time.

Or you might notice that the question is now showing up in every area of your life. In your work, your relationships, your body, your rest. And you realize: *this is not going away. This is asking to be taken seriously.*

The threshold is crossed when you finally stop calling it a phase and start calling it a truth.

That moment is both terrifying and oddly relieving. Because you are finally giving voice to something that has been inside you all along.

📖 ✧ Tale vignette – Part One: The Question That Wouldn't Leave

A professional with a stable career hears the same thought every Sunday night: "Whose life am I actually living?" She dismisses it as dramatic, then as selfish, then as a cliché. Weeks turn into months. The question keeps coming back, unchanged.

One day she realizes it is not demanding an immediate answer. It is simply demanding to be taken seriously.

📖 ✧ Tale vignette – Part Two: After the Answer Was Heard

She stops trying to silence the question and instead sits with it. She asks herself: Who decided what this life should look like? Who decided that this job, this status, this version of success is what I should want? And if I am honest—is it what I actually want?

The answers surprise her. Not because they are dramatic, but because they are clear. And once she has answered them honestly, she cannot un-hear the answers.

◆ A Deeper Look: The Wisdom of Persistent Questions

Persistent questions are not glitches in your system. They are features. They are your inner wisdom speaking to you in the only language that will eventually get your attention.

Your mind can ignore a single thought. But a question that returns again and again, that resurfaces in different contexts, that refuses to be dismissed—that is your deepest self-insisting that you pay attention.

The question is not trying to make your life harder. It is trying to help you live a life that is aligned with who you are.

◆ Questions to Carry with You

What question keeps visiting you, no matter how much you try to ignore, distract, or explain it away?

Say it aloud. Give it words. What is the question you have been avoiding?

How have you been minimizing or pathologizing it?

What story have you told yourself about why this question does not matter? Why you should not be asking it? Why you are bad for asking it?

What would it mean to treat that question as an invitation instead of a threat?

Not to immediately answer it. Just to sit with it. To take it seriously. What would change?

If the answer to this question requires you to change something about your life, what is the first thing that would have to shift?

Not everything. Just the first thing.

Who would be upset or disappointed if you answered this question honestly?

And whose responsibility is that disappointment? Is it your job to prevent it?

What would become possible if you finally gave this question the attention it has been asking for?

What might you discover? What might you become?

Threshold 8 – Recognition, Facing the Moment Where Excuses No Longer Fit

Recognition, here, means finally seeing that the stories you have been using to stay the same are not facts about the world, but excuses you have outgrown.

There comes a point when the reasons you have given yourself for staying the same begin to feel thin. The stories that once comforted you "It's not the right time," "People like me do not do that," "I do not have a choice"—start to sound rehearsed.

This threshold is the honest recognition: "These are not facts. These are excuses I've outgrown."

◆ The Landscape of Comfortable Excuses

Excuses are not lies, exactly. They are true stories that are no longer complete.

They were true once. The circumstance really was difficult. The timing really was wrong. You really did not have the resources or the support or the clarity you needed.

But circumstances change. Timing shifts. Resources become available. Support arrives. Clarity emerges.

And the excuses that were once honest explanations become comfortable shields.

The reason this happens is that excuses work. They keep you safe. They give you permission to stay where you are. They explain your choices to yourself and to others in a way that makes you sound reasonable.

I cannot leave this job because I need the money.

I cannot end this relationship because I am afraid of being alone.

I cannot pursue that dream because I have responsibilities.

I cannot be honest because it will hurt people.

I cannot take care of myself because everyone else needs me.

All of this might be true. But the question is: are they still true? Or have they become comfortable stories that let you avoid the discomfort of choosing?

◆ What Excuse-Making Looks Like in Different Contexts

In career:

"I cannot leave this job because I need the money." And that is true. You do need the money. But let us look closer. How much money do you need? And how much are you making? Are you leaving enough on the table to stay, or are you using the money as an excuse to not have to make a harder choice about what you want to do?

In relationships:

"I cannot be honest because it will hurt them." And maybe it will. But is that your responsibility? Is it your role to protect everyone else from the reality of your feelings? And at what cost to yourself?

In health:

"I cannot take care of myself because everyone else needs me." And they might need you. But what if you are not actually helping them by sacrificing yourself? What if the most helpful thing you could do is model how to take care of yourself?

In creativity:

"I cannot pursue this because I am too old / too late / too out of practice." But is that true? Or is it an excuse that feels safer than trying?

In dreams:

"I cannot do that because I do not have the education / experience / talent / connections." And you do not. Right now. But could you get them? Would you get them if you decided to?

◆ The Moment Excuses Stop Working

Excuses stop working when reality no longer supports them.

You might realize I have been saying I cannot leave this job for five years. But the economic situation has changed. I have savings now. The market is better. The excuse is not as solid as it used to be.

Or: I have been saying it is not the right time for ten years. But there will never be the "right time." I have been using time as an excuse to not choose.

Or: I have been saying I do not have a choice. But that is not true. I have choices. I just do not like any of them. And I have been confusing "I do not like my choices" with "I do not have choices."

The moment is uncomfortable because it is the moment you can no longer hide behind the excuse. You can no longer tell yourself a story that feels completely honest.

You must acknowledge I have a choice. I just do not want to make it. Because the choice is hard.

◆ The Resistance You Will Feel

When your excuses begin to lose their power, the resistance is both quiet and fierce.

Your comfort says:

"But I have built a life around this excuse. If I let go of it, everything will have to change."

Your fear says:

"If I do not have an excuse, then I am responsible. And I do not want to be responsible for this choice."

Your doubt says:

"My excuse is legitimate. I really do not have a choice. Maybe I am just being dramatic."

Your loyalty says:

"If I stop using this excuse, people will judge me. They will think I am selfish."

All these voices are protecting you from the vulnerability of claiming your own choices.

But here is the truth: you have always had a choice. You have just been making the choice not to choose. And there is a difference between "I cannot" and "I am choosing not to because the cost of choosing feels too high."

◆ The Moment the Threshold Becomes Visible

The moment usually arrives when you hear yourself repeating the same excuse for the hundredth time.

You might be talking to a friend, or to a therapist, or to yourself—and you hear yourself saying the same thing you have been saying for years. And something in your register: *Wait. I have been saying this for a very long time. And nothing has changed. Because I have not changed. Because I have been using this excuse to not have to change.*

Or someone might ask you, gently: "But what if you did choose? What would happen?"

And you realize: you do not actually know. You have spent so long explaining why you cannot choose that you have never sat with what would happen if you did.

The threshold is crossed when you finally admit: These are not facts. These are stories I have been telling myself. And I am ready to tell myself a different story.

📖 ✧ Tale vignette – Part One The Story He Kept Telling

A man hears himself, yet again, telling a friend, "You do not understand, I cannot change—my situation is different." The friend nods kindly and lets it go. Later that night, alone in his kitchen, he realizes he has been giving the same speech for years while his actual circumstances have changed significantly.

The one thing that has not moved is his willingness to choose.

📖 ✧ Tale vignette – Part Two: When Possibility Became Responsibility

He sits with an uncomfortable question: What if I stopped using my situation as an excuse and asked myself: what do I want? What would I choose if I gave myself permission?

The answers frighten him. Not because they are impossible, but because they are possible. And if they are possible, then he must choose. And if he chooses, he is responsible.

And that responsibility—to himself—is what he has been avoiding all along.

◆ A Deeper Look: The Cost of Staying in Excuses

There is a research concept called the "intention-behavior gap"—the gap between what we say we want and what we actually do. This gap is not about willpower. It is about permission.

As long as you have an excuse, you do not have to give yourself permission to change. The excuse does the work for you. It explains your choice to yourself and to others in a way that makes you sound reasonable.

But the cost of staying in the excuse is the cost of never becoming. Of never trying. Of never knowing what might be possible if you chose.

◆ Questions to Carry with You

Which explanations about your life have you repeated so often they sound like script lines?

What story have you been telling? How many times have you told it?

Are all of them still completely true—or have some become a shield that lets you stay still?

Be honest. Has your situation changed, even a little?

If you could not use your three favorite excuses, what options would suddenly become visible?

What would you do if you took the excuse away?

What is the real reason you have not chosen yet?

Not an excuse. The real reason. Is it fear? Is it loyalty to someone else? Is it comfort?

What would it feel like to claim responsibility for your choices instead of blaming circumstances?

Not blame yourself. But acknowledge: this is mine to decide.

If you made one different choice this week, just one—what is the smallest change that would be possible?

What could you do if you stopped using the excuse?

Threshold 9 – Remembering You Can Choose Yourself

This threshold is not a single moment; it is a series of small, accumulating recognitions:

You remember that saying yes is supposed to include you. You remember that saying no is allowed, even if no one else understands. You remember that your life is not just something happening to you—it is something you are continually authoring.

At first, these are fragile thoughts. They feel almost impolite in the face of everything and everyone you care about. But the more you let them stand, the more solid they become.

◆ The Landscape of Self-Choice

Self-choice is not the same as selfishness.

Selfishness is taking without considering impact. Self-choice is deciding what you will and will not do, knowing that your decisions will affect others, and choosing to do it anyway.

The difference is that selfishness is unconscious. Self-choice is conscious. You are aware of the impact. You are aware that someone might be disappointed or hurt. And you choose anyway—not out of cruelty, but out of respect for yourself.

This is radical in its simplicity, and radical in its difficulty.

Most people have learned that choosing themselves is inherently selfish. They have internalized the idea that a good person is someone who prioritizes other people's needs above their own. That love means sacrifice. That responsibility means self-erasure.

But there is a paradox hidden in this belief: the people who sacrifice themselves completely end up with nothing to give. The people who prioritize everyone else eventually have nothing left for themselves. The people who say yes to everything end up saying yes to a life that does not feel like theirs.

Self-choice is the recognition that you cannot actually show up fully for anyone if you are running on empty. That the most responsible thing you can do is protect your own aliveness. That saying no is sometimes the most loving thing you can do, because it is the most honest.

◆ What Self-Choice Looks Like in Different Contexts

In time and attention:

You have been saying yes to every request for your time and attention. Your calendar is full of other people's priorities. Your energy is spent on other people's needs. And you say yes because saying no feels impossible, feels selfish, feels like it would hurt people.

But self-choice means asking: *What time do I need for myself? What attention do I need to give to my own life?* And then protecting that time fiercely, the way you would protect time for someone you love.

In relationships:

You have been accommodating, flexible, understanding. You have not asked for what you need because asking feels demanding. You have accepted less than you deserve because accepting more felt like too much.

Self-choice means saying: I need this. And I am going to ask for it. And if you cannot give it to me, that is information about our relationship.

In work:

You have been over-functioning, taking on extra projects, staying late, being available. You have done this because you feared what would happen if you didn't—you would be seen as not committed, not dedicated, not enough.

Self-choice means asking: *What is my actual capacity? What am I willing to give? What do I need in return?* And then protecting those boundaries, even if it means disappointing people.

In creativity and passion:

You have postponed the things that make you feel alive because they are not practical, not productive, not what you are "supposed" to be doing.

Self-choice means making space for what makes you feel alive, even if no one else thinks it is important. Even if it does not produce income or status or approval.

In honesty:

You have been editing your truth to make others comfortable. You have softened your opinions, hidden your feelings, pretended agreement when you disagree.

Self-choice means speaking your truth, knowing that it might make people uncomfortable. Knowing that they might not like it. And doing it anyway because your truth is yours to speak.

◆ **The Liberation and the Discomfort**

Self-choice is oddly liberating.

When you finally give yourself permission to choose yourself, something inside relaxes. The constant work of managing everyone else's feelings, anticipating everyone else's needs, making sure everyone else is okay—that work stops. And it is exhausting work.

But it is also deeply uncomfortable.

Because when you start choosing yourself, people notice. And they may not like it. Your mother might feel hurt that you are not available whenever she wants you. Your partner might feel frustrated that you are no longer accommodating every request. Your boss might feel threatened that you are no longer over-functioning. Your friend might feel abandoned that you are no longer always there.

And you have to sit with that discomfort. You have to let people feel whatever they feel about your choice. You have to resist the urge to explain, justify, or soften the impact.

This is the hard part of self-choice. It is not the choosing itself. It is the allowing others to respond to your choice without trying to manage their response.

◆ The Resistance You Will Feel

When you first begin to practice self-choice, the resistance is immediate and overwhelming.

Your guilt says:

"How can you be so selfish? Look at everything people have done for you. Look at everything they need from you."

Your fear says:

"If you choose yourself, people will leave. They will judge you. They will think you are a bad person."

Your loyalty says:

"You are betraying the people who depend on you. You are breaking a promise you made."

Your doubt says:

"Maybe you do not deserve to choose yourself. Maybe your needs are not as important as everyone else's."

All of these voices are protecting you from the vulnerability of claiming your own life. But what they do not tell you is that they are also protecting you from freedom.

◆ The Moment the Threshold Becomes Visible

The moment usually arrives very quietly.

You might be in a situation where you would normally automatically say yes, and instead you pause. You notice: *I do not actually want to do this. And I am allowed to say no.*

Or someone might ask you to do something, and instead of immediately complying, you find yourself saying, "I need to think about that." And you actually think about it. And you discover: *I do not want to. And that is enough.*

Or you might be in a conversation where you would normally agree, and instead you find yourself saying, "Actually, I disagree." And nothing catastrophic happens. The person is not happy, but they do not leave. The world does not end.

The threshold is crossed when you finally understand: My consent matters. My needs matter. My life is not just something that happens to me, I am authoring it.

That recognition is both powerful and terrifying. Because it means you can no longer blame circumstances. You are responsible. And responsibility is the price of freedom.

📖 ✧ Tale vignette – Part One: The First Time She Meant It

After years of automatic yeses, a woman hears herself say, "I need to think about that," and actually means it. She doesn't commit on the spot. She goes home, sits quietly, and asks, "Do I want this? Do I have capacity? Is this aligned with who I am becoming?"

When she returns with a gentle but firm no, nothing dramatic happens. The world does not end. But something begins: the sense that her life might finally include her.

📖 ✧ Tale vignette – Part Two: What Remained When She Chose Herself

Over the following weeks, she practices this in small ways. A request she would normally accommodate, she says no to. A conversation where she would normally smooth things over, she speaks her truth. A choice she would normally defer to someone else, she makes for herself.

And she discovers something: the people who love her do not leave. They adjust. And the ones who cannot adjust were never really loving her anyway—they were loving the version of her that existed to serve them.

Choosing herself does not end her relationships. It clarifies them.

◆ A Deeper Look: The Neuroscience of Self-Care

When you are constantly in service to other people—when your nervous system is always oriented toward their needs, their emotions, their comfort, your own nervous system never gets to regulate. You are always in a state of mild activation, always scanning for what others need, always managing yourself in relation to them.

Self-choice—saying no, setting boundaries, protecting time for yourself—is not selfish. It is necessary for your nervous system to regulate. It is how you return to baseline. It is how you restore your capacity to actually be present and helpful when you are with other people.

The paradox is: the more you choose yourself, the more you have to give. The more you set boundaries, the more present you can be within those boundaries. The more you protect your own aliveness, the more alive you are for everyone around you.

◆ Questions to Carry With You

Where in your life have you been absent from your own decisions, letting momentum or expectation decide for you?

Where have you said yes when you meant no? Where have you gone along when you wanted to go a different direction?

What does it mean, concretely, to "choose yourself" in one small situation this week?

Not a big, dramatic choice. Just one small moment where your consent matters.

How would your days begin to look different if you acted as if your inner consent mattered as much as anyone else's expectations?

What would shift? What would feel different?

What are you afraid would happen if you said no? Be specific. Name the fear.

Who would be most upset if you started choosing yourself?

And whose job is it to manage their upset? Is it yours?

What would become possible if you finally trusted that you are allowed to have a life that includes you?

What would you do? What would you say? What would you protect?

How These Thresholds Are Really Crossed

These nine inner thresholds are not tasks to complete. They are places to notice.

You do not cross them by force.

You cross them by telling the truth about where you are drifting, disappearing, postponing, performing, surviving, excusing, and, finally, remembering.

Every principle that follows grows out of these quiet, powerful recognitions.

A Life Witness

You have crossed nine thresholds. You have seen where you are drifting, disappearing, postponing, performing, surviving, and excusing yourself from your own life.

Recognition is not the same as change—but it is where change begins.

What follows is the story of a woman who crossed these thresholds and then did the hardest thing: she moved. She didn't stay stuck in understanding. She didn't analyze herself into paralysis. She saw—and then she acted, imperfectly, courageously, one small choice at a time.

After her story, you will find a warning about what happens when people do not move—when they stay trapped in reflection without action. And then, the principles that show you how to bridge seeing and becoming.

But first: witness what's possible when you choose to come back.

📖 She Came Back to Herself

For a long time, her life moved on rails she didn't build but felt responsible for keeping polished.

She worked in an office where the lights came on before the sun did. Emails, deadlines, forms, signatures, she could do it all almost without thinking. People relied on her because she got things done and rarely complained. If you asked anyone, they would say she was steady, dependable, the kind of person who remembered birthdays and emergencies in equal measure.

At home, she raised four kids. Each one different, each one needing something only she seemed to know how to give. She packed lunches, signed forms, drove everyone everywhere, listened to every story, and sat beside beds late at night when someone couldn't sleep. She didn't think of it as sacrifice. To her, it was just an ordinary day.

Her husband had been kind once, and then tired, and then suddenly not there anymore. Loss doesn't always arrive with fanfare—sometimes it just takes the air out of the room and leaves you to figure out how to breathe again. She didn't crumble. There wasn't time.

So, she became everything.

She paid the bills. She made decisions. She did the quiet work of being the person who keeps things from falling apart. People told her she was strong and resilient, but what they didn't see was that strength sometimes just meant not having any other option.

Eventually she stopped asking herself what she wanted. Wanting felt extravagant. She learned to measure her days in what got done, not in what she felt. It became easier that way.

She didn't think of herself as lonely. She thought of herself as busy.

And when people suggested dating again, she smiled and shook her head. "No," she'd say. "That part of my life is closed." She meant it.

Time did what time always does: the children grew up.

One moved across the country. One started working long hours. One was still figuring life out. One drifted in and out between school, friends, plans that changed. They all loved her, but they no longer needed her in the same all-consuming way they once had.

The house didn't feel empty. Just rearranged.

There were evenings now where nobody asked for a ride or advice or dinner at a particular time. She would walk through the rooms and realize the rhythm of the house no longer beat around her. She had space, and with it came a strange, unexpected question: What do I do now?

People suggested clubs or classes or picking up something "just for you." She tried to answer politely, but the truth was simpler and heavier: She wasn't sure what she liked anymore. When you spend years shaping yourself around other people's needs, your own preferences fade like writing left in the rain.

She told everyone she was fine. She said it so often it took on the shape of a fact.

He arrived in her life quietly.

They met through mutual friends, the way people do in ordinary settings that do not feel like turning points at the time. They talked in that easy way where conversation doesn't feel like effort. Days became messages. Messages became coffee. Coffee became something she didn't know she'd missed.

He didn't rush her. He didn't try to fix her. He simply made room.

She found herself laughing at things that weren't practical. She noticed she had opinions again about music, food, evenings, and places. She noticed she was thinking in terms of what she wanted, not just what was needed.

It wasn't that she became someone new. It was that someone familiar stepped back into the light.

The people around her noticed the shift, each in their own way.

Some simply smiled because she seemed lighter.

Others had to adjust to the new emotional reality. There were pauses sometimes when she mentioned plans. Occasional changes in tone. Not anger. Just uncertainty about what it all meant.

Among the children, responses varied.

One was happily distant and supportive from afar. One shrugged and said, "I'm glad you are happy." One watched closely, trying to understand the new balance. One sometimes pulled away for a while, then returned, then stepped back again—like learning to stand in waves.

There were also protective questions asked gently, and sometimes less gently. Not because they wanted to take anything from her, but because they had spent so long seeing her be hurt and tired that caution felt safer than celebration.

They needed time. So did she.

She kept loving them. She kept showing up.

But she stopped vanishing into the background of her own life.

She realized love didn't require her to shrink. She learned that she could care for the people she loved deeply and also protect a space for herself without it being betrayal. The peace didn't come from convincing anyone to understand. The peace came from knowing she didn't have to disappear anymore.

She once believed that the best years of her life were behind her—the ones where she was indispensable and exhausted and always on the verge of running out of time.

Now she knows something quieter and truer: She had not stopped being herself. She had only stepped aside from her own life for a while.

She is not trying to be twenty again, or someone different, or someone new.

She is simply back.

Back to laughing without permission. Back to believing joy doesn't have to be justified. Back to occupying her life fully instead of carefully.

And this time, she intends to stay.

♦ A Deeper Look: When Survival Consumes Time

Time is the most valuable asset a human being has. It does not renew. It does not pause. And it does not announce when it is being spent in ways that cannot be recovered.

Most people do not give their time away recklessly. They give it away responsibly. To children. To work. To family. To keeping life functioning. In long seasons of survival, time is not experienced as something you *have*. It is something you *use*—carefully, efficiently, for everyone else.

When responsibility is constant, there is rarely space to ask what that time is costing you. Days are measured in what gets done, not in what is nourished. Years pass this way—not because you are careless with your life, but because taking care of yourself feels less important than tending to everything that depends on you.

Over time, self-care stops feeling optional and starts feeling indulgent. Rest feels postponable. Joy feels unnecessary. Wanting feels extravagant. The assumption becomes subtle but firm: *I will return to myself later.*

But time does not wait for later.

This is not a moral failure. It is a structural one. When survival stretches on for years, the self is not actively abandoned—it is deferred. Again and again. Until deferral becomes habit, and habit becomes identity.

Many people only realize the cost when the demands finally ease— when children grow up, when crises end, when the calendar opens. By then, years have passed. Not wasted. Lived fully for others. But lived without protection for the one life that could never be replaced.

The work of returning to yourself is not about reclaiming lost time. That is impossible.

It is about honoring the time that remains.

Because choosing yourself is not selfish. It is how you stop spending the most valuable asset you have without ever including yourself in the return.

PART III
THE SPACE BETWEEN

Why Insight Alone Is Not Enough

Understanding can feel like movement.

It is not.

This part exists for the space where people stall—
where clarity grows but life stays the same.

Here, you meet the tension

between knowing and living,

between insight and embodiment,

between who you have been and who you are becoming.

Chapter Three

BETWEEN SEEING
AND BECOMING

You have crossed nine thresholds. You have seen where you drift, where you disappear, where you perform and postpone and excuse yourself from your own life.

And now—right here, in this moment—there is a particular kind of trap waiting.

You can see your life clearly. You understand the patterns. You recognize the costs. And you might be tempted to stay in that place of understanding, waiting for something to shift.

But reflection without action becomes its own form of paralysis.

You become very good at seeing. Very good at naming what is wrong. Very good at understanding why you are stuck. You read about change. Your journal about change. You talk about change. You think deeply about change.

And nothing changes.

In fact, something worse happens: you become depressed about the fact that nothing is changing. You become resentful that you can see the problem but cannot seem to solve it. You become envious of people who seem to have moved past this stage into actual transformation. You become stuck in a different way—stuck in the knowledge that your life is not working without yet having the courage to do anything about it.

This chapter is about that particular cost. The cost of waking up without acting. The cost of seeing without changing. The cost of understanding without embodying.

◆ The Psychology of Reflection Without Action

When you finally see your life clearly—when you cross those first thresholds, when you recognize the patterns—something shifts neurologically.

Your brain becomes activated around the problem. You start noticing things you never noticed before. You begin to understand the roots of your patterns. You see how the pieces connect. You recognize the cost of how you have been living.

This is good. This is necessary. But here is what research on behavior change shows: awareness alone is not enough.

Awareness can actually become a trap.

When you become aware of a problem without taking action to solve it, something called the "intention-behavior gap" widens. You become hyperaware of the discrepancy between what you know you should do and what you are actually doing. You notice the gap constantly. And the more you notice it, the more uncomfortable it becomes.

But instead of using that discomfort as fuel for action, you can use it as fuel for more reflection. You think, "If I just understand it more deeply, then I will be able to change." So, you read more. You journal more. You analyze more. You spiral deeper into understanding.

And the gap widens further.

Because understanding is not the same as changing. And at a certain point, more understanding becomes a form of avoidance.

◆ The Four Stages of Reflection Without Action

Stage One: Recognition and Relief

You finally see it. Something inside you says: "Yes, that is it. That is why I have been feeling this way." And there is relief in recognition. For the first time, the experience has a name. The pattern has a shape. And that shape feels manageable somehow—because at least now you understand it.

You might feel hopeful. You might think: "Now that I see this, I can change it."

Stage Two: Deeper Understanding

You start to understand not just the pattern, but the roots of the pattern. You trace it back to childhood, to family dynamics, to old decisions you made about who you needed to be in order to survive. You understand how intelligent the pattern was, how it kept you safe, how it made sense given what you knew at the time.

This deepening understanding feels like progress. But it is also becoming a form of self-protection. Because if you understand why, you are the way you are, you do not have to change it, you just have to feel compassionate about it. And compassion, while important, is not the same as change.

Stage Three: Frustration and Resentment

You have now been aware of the pattern for a while. You understand it deeply. And yet—you are still doing it. You still catch yourself drifting, disappearing, performing, surviving. And recognition is no longer relief; it is frustration.

You think things like: "I know better. Why am I still doing this?" or "I understand the pattern. Why can't I just stop it?"

The frustration builds because you are measuring yourself against an impossible standard: the standard of someone who knows better and therefore should be better immediately.

And when you are not better immediately, you begin to resent the pattern. You resent yourself for the pattern. You resent other people who seem to have figured this out and moved on. You resent the fact that seeing the problem does not automatically solve it.

Stage Four: Depression and Stuckness

If you stay in reflection without action long enough, something shifts from frustration to something heavier.

Depression arrives. Not necessarily clinical depression, though that is possible. But a kind of existential depression—the sense that you can see your life is not working, you understand why it is not working, and yet you seem powerless to change it.

You might experience:

A sense of hopelessness: "I see the problem, but I cannot fix it."

A sense of fatigue: "I have been thinking about this for so long and nothing is different."

A sense of disconnection: "I am aware of my life, but I am not actually living it."

A sense of envy: "Other people seem to just move through life without all this thinking and analyzing. Why is it so hard for me?"

A sense of shame: "I should be further along by now. I should be able to change this."

At this stage, reflection has become a trap. You are stuck inside your own understanding, unable to move forward, unable to go back to not knowing.

◆ The Deeper Roots: Attachment and Identity

To understand why reflection without action becomes so sticky, it is helpful to understand some of the psychology underneath.

Attachment theory tells us that in our early relationships, we learned how to be in the world. We learned what was safe, what was dangerous, what earned love, what created distance. These lessons became embedded in our nervous system, and they shape how we move through the world as adults.

When you first become aware of these patterns, something interesting happens you recognize them as patterns. You see that they were learned. You understand that they made sense at the time.

But there is something threatening about this recognition.

Because if these patterns are learned, that means you could learn something different. And learning something different means changing. And changing means stepping into the unknown. And the unknown—even if it is better—is scary.

So, the mind does something intelligent: it keeps reflecting. It keeps analyzing. It keeps trying to understand the pattern more deeply, as if understanding is the thing that will make change safe.

But what you are really doing is buying time. You are staying in a place where you know the terrain, even if the terrain is painful.

◆ Why Recognition Feels Like Betrayal

There is something worth exploring here: the strange feeling that often comes when you finally recognize a pattern.

Sometimes it feels like recognition. Sometimes it feels like relief. But sometimes, especially if the pattern involves people you love, it feels like betrayal.

Because recognizing the pattern means recognizing that someone you love may have contributed to it. Your parents may have taught you to be small. Your partner may have benefited from your disappearance. Your family system may have needed you to be the responsible one.

And recognizing that can feel like a betrayal of loyalty.

You think things like: "If I admit this pattern came from my mother, am I blaming her? Am I being ungrateful? Am I betraying her by seeing her role in it?"

Or: "If I admit my partner benefits from my disappearing, does that mean they are bad? Does that mean I have to leave? Does that mean our relationship is dishonest?"

Or: "If I admit my family system needed me to be the strong one, does that mean I have to stop being strong? Does that mean I abandon everyone?"

These questions can feel so threatening that instead of moving through the recognition into action, you stay in reflection. You try to understand in a way that will not feel like betrayal. You try to find a way to acknowledge the pattern while still being loyal to the people involved.

But loyalty to other people cannot come at the cost of your own integrity. And at a certain point, that understanding has to shift into action.

◆ The Guilt of Waking Up

There is another layer to the stuckness that happens in reflection without action: guilt.

When you start to wake up to your own life, when you start to see the patterns and the costs, you might feel guilty in ways you did not expect.

You might feel guilty that you are only now seeing things that others have been trying to tell you for years. You might feel guilty that you have wasted time, that you have made choices you regret, that you have hurt people through your patterns. You might feel guilty that you are starting to want things for yourself when other people depend on you.

And guilt is a powerful force. It can keep you stuck in reflection as a way of paying penance. As if by continuing to feel bad about the pattern, you are somehow atoning for it.

But guilt without change just perpetuates the pattern. It does not undo the past. It does not help anyone. It just keeps you small, stuck, and suffering.

At a certain point, the most responsible thing you can do is stop feeling guilty and start changing. Not to hurt people, but to honor the fact that you finally see what needs to change.

◆ The Power (and Risk) of Vulnerability

Here's the tricky part:

To remember who you are, you have to be willing to be seen—including by yourself.

That means letting yourself feel things you have pushed down: grief, regret, envy, desire, disappointment, and tenderness. It means admitting, "The life I built might look good, but parts of it do not feel like me."

Researcher Brené Brown has spent years studying this territory. She often says that "vulnerability is the birthplace of innovation, creativity, and change." In other words, if you refuse to be vulnerable, you also quietly refuse growth.

Vulnerability is not oversharing. It's telling the truth, first to yourself, about what is really going on—and letting that truth have consequences.

📖 ✧ Tale vignette –John and the Illusion of Success

John was the kind of man people pointed to and said, "He's made it."

Corner office. Nice car. Impressive title. His calendar was full; his life, supposedly, was too.

If you asked him about happiness, he'd talk about milestones:

When I close this deal. When I hit that number. When I retire.

For years, he carried around an unspoken equation in his head:

success = money + status = happiness

It was simple. It was clean. And it kept him moving.

Then, at a leadership retreat, a speaker asked a question that made him unexpectedly uncomfortable:

"When you were a kid, before anyone expected anything of you, what did you love to do just because it made you come alive?"

John was surprised at what came up: not business, not competition, but cooking.

He remembered being twelve years old, experimenting in his mother's kitchen, mixing flavors just to see what would happen. He remembered the joy on people's faces when they tasted something he'd made. Somewhere along the way, that boy had vanished under budgets and quarterly reports.

He didn't walk out of the seminar and burn his career down. But he did something small and brave: he started cooking again. First on weekends. Then for friends. Then, slowly, he began to imagine a different kind of future.

Years later, that path led him to open a small fusion restaurant—not as an escape from his old identity, but as a place where his outer life and his inner joy could finally sit at the same table.

John's story is not about quitting your job to chase a hobby. It's about refusing to let success be defined for you by people who do not have to live your life.

What Living on Autopilot Costs You

If you stay in reflection without action, if you keep understanding without embodying, keep analyzing without changing—you pay a particular price.

You pay with your time.

Days and weeks and months and years pass. And the pattern is still there. And you have not actually moved forward. You have just become more aware of your stuckness.

You pay with your hope.

Every time you recognize the pattern and do not change it, something inside you loses a little bit of faith that change is possible. You begin to believe that you are fundamentally stuck. That seeing the problem is as close as you can get to solving it.

You pay with your relationships.

People around you begin to lose patience with reflection without action. They watch you talk about change and not change. They listen to you analyze the pattern and continue the pattern. And at a certain point, they may stop believing that change is possible. Or they may leave, unable to watch someone they care about stay stuck.

You pay with your energy.

Reflection without action is exhausting. You are constantly aware of the discrepancy between how you are living and how you want to live. You are constantly managing the discomfort of that gap. And that management takes energy that could go toward actually living.

You pay with your self-respect.

At a certain point, you know you cannot respect yourself for continuing a pattern you have clearly identified. You cannot respect yourself for staying in a situation you have named as damaging. You cannot respect yourself for understanding and not acting.

And the loss of self-respect is perhaps the most dangerous cost of all. Because without self-respect, you lose the foundation that makes change possible.

◆ The Tale of the Woman Who Understood Everything

📖 ✧ Tale vignette – The Woman in the Mirror

For two years, Sarah read everything about her patterns. She went to therapy. She journaled. She analyzed her childhood. She understood, with stunning clarity, exactly why she disappeared in relationships, why she said yes when she meant no, why she had built a life around being useful to everyone else.

She could explain it all. She could trace each pattern back to its origin. She could see how her mother's anxiety had made her become calm. How her father's disappointment had made her become accomplished. How her brother's neediness had made her become helpful.

She understood it beautifully. Completely. And nothing changed.

She still said yes when she meant no. She still disappeared in relationships. She still built her life around everyone else's needs.

But now she understood why she was doing it. And somehow, that made it worse.

Because understanding without changing meant she could see her own patterns with perfect clarity. She could watch herself do the thing she did not want to do, and she could explain exactly why she was doing it. She could feel herself disappearing and she could name the moment it was happening. And she could not stop it.

One day, after another therapy session where she had articulated her pattern with impressive eloquence, she sat in her car in the parking lot and felt something shift. Not into hope. Into anger.

She thought: "I have spent two years understanding this. I have talked about it in every conversation. I have analyzed it from every angle. I have become very good at seeing myself clearly. And I am still here. Still doing the same thing. Still stuck."

And at that moment, she realized: understanding had become a way of staying stuck. The more she understood, the more she could explain her stuckness. The more she analyzed, the more proof she had that the pattern was deep, old, reasonable.

And as long as understanding was the goal, she never had to move toward change. She never had to take the risk of actually doing something different.

That was the moment something shifted. Not because she suddenly had a magical insight. But because she finally got tired of being insightful.

She stopped going to therapy for a while. She stopped journaling. She stopped analyzing. And in the silence, a different question emerged: "What if I just tried something different, even though I do not fully understand why I need to? Even though I am afraid. Even though it might not work?"

She did not have all the answers. But she started moving anyway.

◆ A Word About Depression, Resentment, and Envy

If you find yourself in this stage—where you can see your patterns clearly but cannot seem to change them, it is important to name what you might be feeling.

Depression in this context might feel like: "What is the point? I see the problem. I understand it. I cannot fix it."

But depression at this stage is not a sign that you cannot change. It is a sign that you are ready to change. Your system is telling you: this understanding is no longer enough. You need to move.

Resentment might feel like: "Why is this so hard for me? Why do other people just move forward without all this struggle?"

But resentment is often a sign of a boundary that needs to be set. In this case, the boundary might be: "I am not going to spend all my energy understanding this. I am going to spend some of my energy doing something about it."

Envy of people who seem to have figured this out might feel like: "They do not seem to struggle with this the way I do. They just change and move on."

But envy is information. It is telling you: this is what is possible. This is what I want. This is what I am capable of.

All of these feelings, depression, resentment, envy—are not signs that something is wrong with you. They are signs that you are ready to move.

◆ Questions to Sit With

Where in your life have you been in reflection mode for a long time without moving into action?

What have you been analyzing, journaling about, or understanding without changing?

What are you afraid would happen if you stopped reflecting and started acting?

What is the risk you have been avoiding?

How long have you been aware of a particular pattern?

And what would need to be true for you to finally move toward changing it?

What guilt are you carrying that might be keeping you stuck in reflection?

Whose loyalty are you trying to protect by staying still?

If you gave yourself permission to move imperfectly, to try something different without fully understanding why, what would you try?

What is the smallest action that would be possible?

What would change about your relationship with yourself if you moved from understanding to acting?

How would you feel different if you took just one step?

◆ The Bridge Between Seeing and Becoming

This chapter exists because the gap between seeing your life clearly and actually changing it is real—and it is dangerous.

You can become highly sophisticated in your understanding of your own patterns. You can articulate your history, name your wounds, and analyze exactly why you are stuck. And still remain stuck.

The thresholds in Chapter 2 are about seeing. They are about recognition—about naming what is happening in your life with clarity and honesty. That work matters. But if you only see—if you recognize yourself without moving—you eventually enter a different kind of suffering.

You become depressed. Resentful. Envious of people who seem to have moved past this stage. You begin to suffer not from confusion, but from clarity without motion—the pain of understanding your life without changing it.

The principles in Chapter 3 are the bridge.

They are how you move from seeing to becoming. From insight to embodiment. From understanding into lived experience. They are not abstract ideas or philosophical positions. They are daily practices, small choices, and moment-to-moment decisions that translate what you have seen into how you actually live.

But you have to be willing to move.

You have to be willing to step out of reflection and into action—even when you do not have all the answers yet. Even when you are afraid. Even when you cannot fully explain why you are doing it.

Because sometimes change has to come before understanding.

Sometimes you have to try something different and then discover why it works.

You have crossed the thresholds. You have done the recognition work. You understand your patterns with clarity.

Now comes the harder, quieter work.

You are ready.

What follows is how.

PART IV
LIVING FROM INNER CONSENT

Choosing Yourself in Real Life

This is where life answers back.

Choosing yourself is not a declaration.

It is a practice—

tested by relationships, routines, fear, and doubt.

This part is about living honestly inside the ordinary pressures of real life and **learning to return to yourself** again and again.

Chapter Four

SEVEN PRINCIPLES FOR LIVING ON PURPOSE

There Is a Difference Between Waking Up and Knowing How to Live It

Seeing the truth about your life and knowing how to live from that truth are not the same thing.

You have crossed thresholds already. You have noticed where you drift instead of deciding, where you disappear instead of arriving, where you postpone yourself, perform, survive, excuse, and, finally, remember. You have tasted the strange relief of honesty and the discomfort that comes with it.

But recognition, by itself, can be disorienting.

You see more clearly, yet your days may still look the same. You understand your patterns, yet you still catch yourself repeating them. You know that "later" has turned into "never," yet you are not sure what to do today instead. Waking up has happened; knowing how to live awake is still unfolding.

This is where principles matter.

Thresholds say, "This is what you are finally seeing."

Principles say, "This is how you can begin to live from what you see."

You are not broken for not knowing how to do that yet.

No one is born knowing how to build a life around inner truth instead of outer expectation. Most people never even get to the point of seeing the difference. The fact that you are here means you already have what matters most: awareness.

Now you need a way to move with it.

What a Principle Is (Not a Rule, But a Way of Relating)

A principle is not a rule to obey.

Rules say:

- Do this, do not do that.

- Always, never, should, must.

Rules collapse complexity into instructions. They might work for a while, but they eventually break under the weight of real life.

A principle is different.

A principle is a way of **relating** to yourself and your life that holds true across situations, even when the details change. It does not tell you exactly what to do. It changes the place you move *from*.

"See yourself before you try to fix yourself" doesn't dictate a script. It changes how you approach every moment of self-improvement.

"Choose values that feel like home" doesn't tell you which job to take. It changes how you weigh every decision.

"Align your days with your inner consent" doesn't say yes or no for you. It changes who gets to decide.

Principles give you a center, not a checklist.

You will not apply them perfectly. That is not their purpose. Their purpose is to slowly shift your default—away from self-attack, borrowed values, drifting, survival, performance, and disappearance, and toward a life that feels like it is actually yours.

Think of each principle as a way of holding the steering wheel rather than a specific route on the map.

The Rhythm You'll Notice in Each Principle

Each principle in this part follows a rhythm on purpose. The rhythm is there to keep you out of self-attack and inside honest, sustainable change.

You will notice four movements:

First: Naming the cost of how you have been living. Each principle begins by telling the truth about what it costs you to keep doing things the old way—how self-attack wears you down, how borrowed values leave you empty, how drifting drains your sense of power, how survival erases you, how certain relationships shrink you, how avoiding discomfort keeps you stuck, how ignoring your inner consent makes your days feel like they belong to someone else. This is not to shame you. It is to help you see clearly enough that you stop calling pain "just how it is."

Then: Offering a different way of relating to yourself. Before any action steps, each principle gives you a new posture: seeing before striving, aligning instead of performing, choosing instead of drifting, living instead of only surviving, staying true instead of shrinking, learning from discomfort instead of fleeing it, acting with consent instead of obligation.

Without this shift in how you relate to yourself, any practical change will quietly turn back into self-attack.

Then: A story that shows the principle in motion. Each principle includes a tale life in miniature—so you can feel the principle, not just think it. You meet people who do what you do: make lists and break them, live by borrowed scripts, say "I have no choice," survive too well, disappear in relationships, avoid boundaries, say yes while meaning no. The stories are not models of perfection. They are witnesses to what it looks like when an ordinary person tries to live a little more honestly.

Finally: A small practice—less a program, more a doorway. At the end of each principle, you'll find questions to sit with.

Not a ten-step plan. Not a performance test. Just a few focused questions designed to tilt your attention:

toward the small decisions that are already available to you,

toward the moments where you can practice this principle in the life you have now.

You do not have to master any principle to begin. You are not being asked to turn your entire life upside down by next Tuesday.

You are being invited to experiment with a gentler assumption:

You were never broken.

You were never meant to be fixed.

You were meant to be known.

These principles are simply ways of relating to yourself as someone worth knowing—and then letting your days, slowly and imperfectly, begin to reflect that truth.

Principle 1 – Know Yourself First

Most people try to change by turning on themselves.

The inner monologue is predictable:

I should have more discipline.

I should be more thankful.

I should be braver.

I should already have my life figured out.

Beneath all of that is a hard, simple belief:

If I can find enough things wrong with me and attack them relentlessly, maybe I'll finally turn into someone I can live with.

◆ The cost of self-attack

You become project manager of your own inadequacy. Every feeling is a problem to be solved. Every human limitation is treated as a defect. Every setback is taken as proof that you are, at your core, not enough.

For a while, this can even look productive. Self-criticism sometimes creates short bursts of motivation, new routines, strict plans, intense promises to yourself. But underneath, it quietly builds a belief that your worth is always one improvement away. Over time, that belief erodes confidence, increases stress, and makes it harder to try again when you inevitably fall short.

When you relate to yourself this way, change starts to feel like self-erasure. You are not becoming more yourself; you are trying to get rid of yourself.

There is another way to begin.

Seeing before striving.

✦ Letting Understanding Come Before Editing

To know yourself before you try to change yourself is to pause the reflex that says, "How do I fix this?" and replace it with,

"What is actually happening in me?"

Not: How do I stop being so sensitive?

But: What happens in me when I feel hurt—and why does it matter so much?

Not: How do I become more productive?

But: What truly energizes me, and what quietly drains me, regardless of what I think "should" work?

Not: How do I stop feeling like too much or not enough?

But: Where did I first learn that my size, my needs, my feelings were a problem?

This kind of seeing is not passive. It is precise. It asks you to notice patterns instead of attacking symptoms. It asks for curiosity instead of condemnation.

Psychology holds a strange, beautiful paradox: people become more capable of changing when they learn to see themselves with less judgment and more compassionate awareness. When you stop treating every flaw as a piece of evidence against you, your defenses loosen and you become more truthful with yourself. And it is that honesty—not pressure—that makes change last.

✦ A Story: Maya Forgets Herself

Let's start with a simple story.

Maya grew up in a family where academic excellence was treated like a survival skill. Her parents were loving—but their love often came wrapped in report cards.

An A meant a celebration.

A B meant a lecture.

Anything lower meant silence at dinner.

By the time she was twelve, "smart and successful" wasn't just a goal. It was her entire identity. Teachers praised her. Relatives introduced her as "our genius." There was always another exam, another competition, another way to prove herself.

What almost no one noticed was the small girl who loved to draw.

Before homework took over, Maya could spend hours sketching in the margins of her notebooks: faces, cities, imagined worlds. Art wasn't a "talent" to her. It was just a way of breathing. But in a house where achievement meant numbers, not colors, drawing slipped quietly into the background.

By the time she started her career, Maya had done everything right. Great school. Strong job. Solid income. People told her she was "set." On paper, she was.

Inside, she felt like she was living someone else's life.

This tension—between outer success and inner hunger—is not unusual. Studies of creative workers and artists in the U.S. show a consistent theme: many feel squeezed by economic and social expectations in ways that can stifle their creativity and authenticity, even as they juggle multiple jobs and pressures to stay afloat.

For Maya, it took almost a decade of waking up tired, going to a job she could do but didn't love, and numbing out at night before a simple question broke through the fog:

"When was the last time I did something just because it delighted me?"

The honest answer? She couldn't remember.

One weekend, almost on a dare to herself, she walked into an art supply store "just to look," and walked out with a sketchbook and a set of pencils. That first evening at the kitchen table, the lines were shaky and the drawings rusty—but something in her exhaled.

She wasn't quitting her job overnight. She wasn't moving to Paris to become a painter. She was simply touching something that felt like hers again.

What changed for Maya over the next year wasn't only her schedule. It was the story she told herself about who she was: not just "the high achiever" but also "the person who sees the world in shapes and shadows and wants to put them on a page."

Reclaiming yourself rarely starts with a grand gesture. It usually starts with one honest question and a tiny act of remembering.

◆ Four Pillars of Rediscovering Yourself

You do not have to use these as steps. Think of them as five "doorways" you can walk through, one at a time, in any order that fits your life.

Recognition — Name what shaped you

Take an honest look at the forces that have molded you: family stories, cultural messages, school, work, religion, social media. Do not blame. Do not sugarcoat. Just name.

What did you have to be to belong?

What parts of you were rewarded?

What parts of you quietly went underground?

You cannot reclaim a self you refuse to see.

Knowing yourself is different from excusing everything you do. It is understanding the conditions to act this way. It is tracing the line from old mirrors and interruptions to current habits and reactions—not so you can blame the past forever, but so you stop fighting shadows and start responding to the real thing.

When you start here, change stops feeling like a battle and starts feeling like alignment. You are no longer trying to become a better version of someone you never chose to be. You are now learning how to live from someone you are only just starting to meet.

Reclamation — Remember what you loved

Think back to earlier versions of you.

What did you do for hours without anyone telling you it was "useful"?

What did you daydream about before you knew what was "practical"?

Maybe it was drawing, like Maya. Maybe it was building things, telling stories, fixing engines, caring for animals, organizing games, taking apart radios.

You do not have to turn any of it into a career. Reclamation is about giving yourself permission to admit: "That was me. That still matters."

Re-invigoration — Put your hands back on what lights you up

Memory alone is not enough. At some point, you have to move from remembering to doing.

Buy the sketchbook.

Sign up for the class.

Join the choir.

Dust off the guitar.

Set aside thirty minutes a week to cook, to write, to learn.

You are not trying to rebuild your entire life in one bold move. You are opening a window and letting some air back in.

Resilience — Expect resistance and keep going anyway

Any time you change the story of who you are, a few things will push back:

your own fear ("Who do you think you are?")

other people's expectations ("But you have always been the reliable one/successful one/caretaker.")

the friction of new habits

This is normal. When you stop playing a role, the people who liked that role may get uncomfortable. When you stop performing for approval, you'll feel the loss of that applause.

Resilience here doesn't mean pretending it doesn't hurt. It means reminding yourself, "The discomfort of being more honest is better than the quiet ache of staying hidden."

The story that follows is about a woman who did what many people do: she spent years trying to improve herself through plans, programs, and promises. Her life was full of lists—most of them unfinished. What shifted her was not a better plan.

It was a different question.

📖 Tale vignette – The Woman Who Kept Making Lists

Sophie's bedside table had become a small graveyard of notebooks.

They all started the same way: a fresh cover, a new pen, and a title at the top of page one.

"Fix My Life – Plan."

"New Habits, New Me."

"This Time for Real."

Underneath, she would write lists. Wake up earlier. Drink more water. Answer emails on time. Call her parents weekly. Say yes less. Meditate. Stop scrolling. Start running. Be more grateful.

Sunday nights were when the lists appeared. Monday mornings they felt possible. By Wednesday, they were smudged with coffee, buried under laundry, or forgotten in the bottom of her bag. By Friday, a familiar sentence floated through her mind: Next week, I will really try.

Sophie assumed this cycle proved something dark about her: that she was lazy, undisciplined, even fundamentally unserious about her own life. The evidence seemed clear. She could see the pattern; she just could not break it. So, she added a quieter, crueler line to the top of every new list, whether she wrote it or not: Try harder. Be better.

One night, sitting on the edge of her bed with yet another notebook open on her knees, she felt more tired than hopeful. She stared at the title she had just written— "Fix My Life – Spring Version"—and, without quite meaning to, drew a line through it.

Her pen hovered over the crossed-out words. For a moment, the blank space underneath felt uncomfortable, like silence in a conversation where she was supposed to fill the air.

Into that small silence, a different sentence arrived. Not polished, not profound. Just honest.

"What is actually happening in me when I break my own promises?"

She wrote it down and stopped.

It was such a simple shift—from "How do I fix this?" to "What is this?"—but the relief was physical. Her shoulders dropped. Her jaw loosened. For the first time, the page in front of her did not feel like a contract she was destined to break, but like a place she might finally tell the truth.

She did not write a plan that night. She wrote observations.

"I say yes to extra work when I'm afraid of being replaced."

"I stay up late scrolling because it's the only time that feels like mine."

"I make ambitious morning routines when I'm ashamed of how tired I already am."

"I break promises to myself the moment someone else wants something."

None of these were solutions. They were small, clear windows into why she kept doing what she was doing.

When she closed the notebook, nothing in her outer life had changed. Her job was the same. Her inbox was still full. The dishes were still in the sink.

But something quiet and irreversible had shifted: for the first time, she was not treating herself as a broken project to manage. She was treating herself as a person to understand.

Days later, when she caught herself reaching for a new "Fix My Life" list, she paused. The question on that earlier page came back: "What is actually happening in me?"

This time, instead of promising she would wake up two hours earlier forever, she wrote one line: "Tonight, I'm going to bed twenty minutes earlier so tomorrow's version of me has a chance."

It was not impressive. It was not dramatic. No one else would ever know. But in that small decision, she felt a difference. She was not trying to force herself into a new personality overnight. She was beginning to respond to herself with understanding.

The lists on her nightstand changed over time. They did not disappear. They became less like verdicts and more like conversations.

The first principle in this book lives in that shift:

Before you strive to change yourself, learn to see yourself.

Reclamation — Remember what you loved

Think back to earlier versions of you.

What did you do for hours without anyone telling you it was "useful"?

What did you daydream about before you knew what was "practical"?

Maybe it was drawing, like Maya. Maybe it was building things, telling stories, fixing engines, caring for animals, organizing games, taking apart radios.

You do not have to turn any of it into a career. Reclamation is about giving yourself permission to admit: "That was me. That still matters."

◆ Questions to Sit With

When you think about "changing your life," do you feel more like a problem to be solved or a person to be understood?

Where have you been making plans to improve yourself without first asking what is really happening in you?

What labels have you put on yourself ("lazy," "undisciplined," "hopeless with follow-through") that might be descriptions of unaddressed fear, exhaustion, or unmet needs?

What would it look like, this week, to replace the question "How do I fix this?" with "What is this trying to show me?" at least once—and simply notice what changes inside you when you do?

Principle 2 – Choosing Values
That Feel Like Home

There comes a point when "living on purpose" stops sounding like a motivational slogan and starts feeling like a quiet ache. You realize you have worked hard, checked boxes, and hit milestones, yet something in you still feels slightly off to the side of your own life. The outer story might read as "success," but the inner experience does not match.

This principle is about that gap.

It is about moving from borrowed scripts—what you were told matters, what seems impressive, what earns approval—to values that feel like home in your actual body. It is about choosing what you stand on, instead of only standing where you were placed.

◆ From Borrowed Scripts to Inner Alignment

Most people do not start with their own values. They start with inherited ones.

Some values are handed to you directly:

Be productive. Be nice. Be strong. Do not make a fuss. Always say yes. Never waste an opportunity.

Others arrive less through words and more through atmosphere: what got praised, what got criticized, what no one ever talked about.

Over time, you build a life around these borrowed scripts. You pursue what is admired, avoid what is frowned upon, and measure yourself against standards you did not actually choose. You may get incredibly good at this. You may even be rewarded for it.

But there is a cost.

When the values you are living by are not sincerely yours, achievement brings only temporary relief. You feel a brief hit of "I did it," followed by a quieter, more unsettling question: "Why doesn't this feel the way it was supposed to?" Life around you look coherent. Life inside you feel misaligned.

This is where inner alignment begins—not with perfect clarity, but with the honest admission: "I am tired of building my days around values that do not feel like mine."

Alignment does not mean your life becomes instantly simple. It means you stop treating your inner discomfort as ingratitude and start treating it as information. Instead of pushing it down with "I should be happy," you ask, "What is this discomfort trying to tell me about what I truly value?"

◆ When "Success" and Truth Do not Match

There is a moment, sometimes small and private, when the word "success" starts to ring hollow. You realize you have been chasing a picture of a good life that looks convincing on paper but does not feel honest in your chest.

It might show up as:

- Hitting a financial, career, or relational milestone and feeling strangely numb instead of fulfilled.

- Catching yourself saying, "I know I'm lucky; I should be grateful," while something in you quietly whispers, "But this is not it."

- Noticing that the things you call "wins" cost you energy, presence, or integrity in ways you can no longer ignore.

In these moments, there is often a split inside: part of you insists, "This is what I'm supposed to want," while another part of you refuses to sign the contract anymore.

The principle here is not that your current life is wrong. It is that your definition of "right" may have been built without your full participation.

When "success" and truth do not match, you are not being ungrateful. You are being invited. The invitation is not necessarily to burn everything down, but to begin asking different questions:

- Instead of "What will people respect?" ask, "What will I respect in myself ten years from now?"

- Instead of "What looks impressive?" ask, "What feels honest, even if no one is watching?"

- Instead of "What keeps the peace?" ask, "What keeps me whole?"

Choosing values that feel like home means you stop outsourcing your definition of a good life and start listening to the part of you that has been quietly, persistently saying, "This matters to me," even when it doesn't match the script.

📖 Tale vignette – The Version That Waited

For most of her thirties, Elena could summarize her life in one sentence: "Everything looks great on paper."

She had the job her parents bragged about, the apartment her friends envied, the calendar full of networking events and weekend plans that made her appear endlessly in demand. When people said, "You are really killing it," she smiled and agreed. It was easier than explaining the truth: she often felt like a visitor in her own days.

On the surface, she was thriving. Underneath, small fractures had begun to show.

She noticed them in quiet places—waiting in line for coffee, on the train home after work, in the elevator ride to her floor. They sounded like simple questions that never quite went away:

"If I stopped needing to impress anyone, would I still choose this?" "Why am I always relieved when something gets canceled?" "When was the last time I felt like myself and not just my role?"

Elena tried to respond the way she had been trained: by working harder. She joined a new committee. She signed up for a leadership program. She said yes to every opportunity that sounded important.

One evening, after a long day of doing exactly what her "five-year plan" version of herself would have approved of, she came home to a quiet apartment, dropped her bag, and sat on the floor. It was late. Her phone was still buzzing with messages. She did not turn on the lights.

On the coffee table was a small, worn notebook from college, something she had grabbed while cleaning earlier and never put away. She reached for it without thinking and flipped it open.

Inside were pages of scribbled ideas for community projects, notes from conversations with friends, questions about what makes people feel at home in their own skin. In the margins, in her younger handwriting, were sentences like:

"I want a life where my work and my values feel like the same language." "I care more about helping people feel seen than about looking impressive." "I never want to lose the part of me that actually listens."

She had written these lines before the job, before the promotions, before the LinkedIn titles and the careful, polished bio. Reading them, she felt a strange mixture of grief and recognition.

"This," she thought, tracing one underlined sentence with her thumb, "is the version of me that waited."

Waited while she prioritized what looked good over what felt true. Waited while she kept saying, "This is just what you do," instead of asking, "But what do I actually value?" Waited in the background while she built a life around borrowed definitions of success.

For the first time, she did not push the feeling away.

She closed her eyes and let the question come fully into focus: "If I believed this younger version of me had something wise to say, what would she ask me to value now?"

The answers were not dramatic. They were specific.

Time for conversations that weren't about work. Space in her week to create and contribute in ways that weren't tied to performance reviews. Integrity in how she used her voice—speaking up when something felt off, even if it made a meeting slightly uncomfortable.

None of these required her to quit her job overnight or move to a cabin in the woods. They required something harder: to let her real values sit at the table when she made decisions.

Over the next months, Elena started experimenting. She stopped automatically saying yes to tasks that only made her look busy. She volunteered for projects that aligned with the things she had written in that old notebook. She began to measure a "good day" less by how impressive it sounded and more by one quiet question: "Did I live any closer to what I say I value?"

Her title did not change. Her email signature did not change. But her experience of her own life did.

The version of her that had been waiting was no longer stuck on the pages of a college notebook. She was finally being invited into the room.

◆ Questions to Sit With

These questions are not a test to pass. They are ways of noticing where you are already leaning toward values that feel like home—and where you may still be living from borrowed scripts.

- When you describe your life as "going well," whose definition of "well" are you using?

- Think of a recent "win" in your life. Did it feel like alignment or like performance—like coming home to yourself, or like holding your breath a little longer?

- What did you quietly value as a younger person—before titles, expectations, or comparisons—that still feels true when you let yourself remember it?

- If you had to choose three values that feel like home in your body (for example: honesty, creativity, steadiness, courage, kindness, freedom, depth), which ones would you name—and where, specifically, do you already live them, even in small ways?

- Where are you currently trading a value that feels like home for a value that mostly earns approval—and what tiny adjustment would move that trade a little closer to your truth this week?

You do not need a perfect list of values to begin living on purpose. You only need to notice, with a little more honesty, which parts of your life feel like you are visiting—and which parts, however small, already feel like home.

Principle 3 – Making Decisions Instead of Drifting

There is a kind of paralysis that does not feel like paralysis. It feels like "going along with what is." You tell yourself that you do not really have a choice, the situation is what it is, the people involved have needs, the timing is not right, the risk is too high. So, you drift, telling yourself you are being reasonable, when what is really happening is that you are avoiding the fact that you are choosing.

This principle is about reclaiming the word "choice" from the moments that feel big and dramatic, and putting it back where it actually lives: in the small, daily decisions you make every time you say yes or no, show up or step back, speak or stay silent.

◆ From "I Have No Choice" to "I Am Choosing"

The phrase "I have no choice" is seductive because it offers relief. If you have no choice, you are not responsible. If you have no choice, whatever happens next is not you are doing. You are simply being carried along by circumstances larger than yourself.

The cost of this belief is enormous.

When you consistently tell yourself you have no choice, you begin to feel powerless in your own life. Resentment builds quietly underneath—not toward the person making demands of you, but toward yourself for accepting a story in which you are passive. Over time, this resentment becomes harder to distinguish from exhaustion. You stop noticing the moments where you actually *do* have a choice, because you have trained yourself to look away from them.

But here is what is true: you have far more choices than you are currently claiming.

Not easy choices. Not choices without consequences. Not choices that will not disappoint someone.

But choices.

You are choosing when you say yes to something because you fear what will happen if you say no. You are choosing when you stay in a situation because it feels less risky than leaving. You are choosing when you prioritize someone else's comfort over your own honesty. You are choosing when you tell yourself a story about why you "cannot" do something you actually could do.

The shift from "I have no choice" to "I am choosing" does not mean you suddenly become selfish or indifferent to other people's needs. It means you stop pretending that your current circumstances are happening *to* you and start admitting that they are happening *because of you*—because of choices you have made, are making, or are refusing to make.

This is where power lives. Not in pretending you have control over everything. But in claiming responsibility for the small decisions that are genuinely yours.

◆ Tiny Decisions That Change Direction

The decisions that matter most are often so small they barely feel like decisions at all.

Not: "Should I leave this job?" (big, dramatic, paralyzing) But: "Will I speak up in this meeting about something I disagree with?" (small, specific, within your control)

Not: "Should I transform my entire relationship?" (overwhelming) But: "Will I tell the truth about how this conversation made me feel, even if it's uncomfortable?" (a real choice, today)

Not: "Will I finally become the person I'm meant to be?" (too abstract) But: "Will I take the class, make the call, have the conversation I've been postponing?" (a concrete choice that has consequences)

Each small decision is a tiny course correction. One choice to speak up does not change everything. But it begins to change something. And when you make one small honest choice, the next one becomes slightly easier to see.

This is how drifting stops. Not through one grand gesture of willpower, but through the accumulation of small decisions where you finally admit: "I am choosing this."

📖 Tale vignette – The Man of No Choice

Marcus had perfected a particular sentence: "I do not really have a choice in this situation."

He said it about his job (too many people depending on him to leave; the market was bad for a transition). He said it about his living situation (his ex-wife needed the house for the kids; he couldn't afford anything else right now). He said it about his time (everyone needed something; he couldn't say no without letting them down). He said it about his marriage (he couldn't be honest about how isolated he felt; it would hurt her too much; what good would that do?).

The narrative was coherent. Marcus was not a victim of malice; he was a victim of circumstances. His life was something that had happened to him, and he was managing it as best he could.

Except, somewhere deep down, he knew it was not true.

The knowledge lived in the quiet moments—driving to work, standing in the shower, lying awake at 3 a.m. In those moments, a smaller voice would whisper, "You could say something. You could ask for something different. You could choose."

But the voice felt irresponsible, so he pushed it down.

One evening, Marcus sat across from his therapist, something he had finally agreed to after his wife mentioned, gently, that he seemed "increasingly absent." During the session, he found himself listing, for the hundredth time, all the reasons he couldn't change anything: the kids needed stability, his wife was already stressed, his job depended on his willingness to be flexible, his mother-in-law would criticize any decision he made.

His therapist listened, then asked a quiet question: "What would it look like if you chose one small thing this week—just one—where you admitted the choice was yours?"

Marcus felt a flash of irritation. "That's not helpful. I do not have—"

"I know," his therapist interrupted gently. "You do not have a choice. I heard that. But let us pretend for a moment that you did. What would be one tiny decision where you could be honest about the fact that *you* are choosing?"

Something in the room shifted. Marcus sat with the question, uncomfortable.

After a long pause, he said quietly, "I could tell her I need to take a walk alone on Sunday mornings instead of spending it running errands together."

"Would that be true?" his therapist asked. "Would that be something you actually want?"

"Yes," Marcus admitted. "But she'll feel hurt. She'll think I do not want to spend time with her."

"Maybe," his therapist said. "But you are currently not spending time with her anyway—you are spending time with her while disappearing. The difference is that in one scenario, you are being honest about the choice you are making."

The words landed strangely. Marcus realized he had gotten so used to the narrative of "I have no choice," he had stopped seeing the moments where he did—and where choosing was, in fact, the more honest path.

That Sunday, Marcus told his wife he wanted to take Sunday mornings for a walk alone. He did not frame it as "I need space from you." He said, "This is something I need for myself to feel more like myself. I'm choosing this."

Her response was not what he had feared. She was quiet for a moment, then asked, "How long have you been in need of this?"

"A while," he admitted.

"Then you should take it," she said. And something in her voice suggested she had been waiting for him to finally claim something as his own.

The Sunday walks did not solve anything overnight. But they changed something. For the first time in years, Marcus spent one hour a week making a choice that was purely his. And once he had claimed that small choice, the next one became visible.

The following week, he found himself actually speaking up in a meeting—disagreeing with a proposal instead of going along with it.

The week after that, he asked his wife a question he had been afraid to ask: "Do you feel like I'm present with you? Because I'm not sure I am."

She didn't say, "No, you are not." She said, "I've been wondering when you'd notice."

These were not dramatic changes. No one's life was transformed. But something had shifted in Marcus. He was no longer drifting and telling himself it was the only way. He was making choices—small ones, honest ones—and admitting they were his.

The voice that had whispered in the shower was finally being listened to.

◆ Questions to Sit With

Where in your life do you use the phrase "I do not have a choice," and is that literally true, or is it a story that lets you avoid responsibility for a difficult decision?

What is one small, specific decision you are currently avoiding by telling yourself you have no choice?

If you admitted that you *are* choosing your current situation—not because you are selfish, but because this choice feels less risky or demanding than the alternative—what would change in how you experience it?

What would become possible if you made one tiny decision this week where you clearly claimed the choice as yours, even if it disappointed someone?

Who might you become if you stopped drifting and started deciding?

Principle 4 – Letting Survival Give Way to Living

There is a season when survival is appropriate. When you are in crisis, in recovery, in the midst of something that requires all your resources just to get through—survival mode is not a character flaw. It is intelligence. It is necessary.

But survival has an insidious way of becoming a permanent address instead of a temporary shelter.

You do so well at surviving—managing the crisis, holding things together, taking care of what needs taking care of—that you forget you were ever allowed to do anything else. And the people around you get so used to you being the one who can handle anything that they stop asking if you are okay. Soon you stop asking yourself.

This principle is about noticing when you have outgrown survival and when it is time to let living begin again—even in small ways, even while some demands still remain.

◆ When Coping Becomes an Identity

Survival looks impressive from the outside. You are the one who gets things done. You are strong, reliable, never asking for anything. You handle crises without falling apart. You are admired for your resilience.

Over time, something quiet happens: surviving becomes who you are.

You start measuring your worth by how much you can endure. Your identity fuses with being the one who copes. Rest starts to feel like laziness. Self-care feels selfish. Taking time for yourself feels irresponsible. You have become so identified with "staying afloat" that the idea of actually *thriving* feels impossible—or worse, undeserved.

This is the cost of letting survival become an identity.

You lose touch with what it feels like to live instead of just manage. Your relationships become transactional—you are the caregiver, the fixer, the one who absorbs everyone else's needs. Tenderness disappears. Spontaneity disappears. You forget what it feels like to do something just because it brings you joy.

The slow tragedy is that while you are busy surviving, the life you could be living quietly passes by.

◆ Making Room for the Self You Postponed

Letting survival give way to living does not require you to stop handling what needs to be handled. It requires you to start asking, "What can I do for myself, even in the midst of what still needs to be managed?"

It might be small.

A walk that no one depends on you for. A conversation with a friend where you talk about something other than the crisis. An hour where you pursue something just because it interests you. A meal cooked slowly instead of efficiently. A book read for no reason other than that you want to read it. Time with yourself where the goal is not productivity but presence.

These are not luxuries. They are reminders that you are not only your obligations. You are someone who deserves to exist outside of what you do for others.

When you start making room for the self you postponed, something shifts. You remember that living is different from surviving. That joy is different from relief. That being present with yourself is not a betrayal of the people who need you; it is a restoration of the person they actually need—someone who is not running on empty.

📖 Tale vignette – The Deferred Self

For seven years, Maria had been the one you called in a crisis.

When her brother lost his job, she helped him restructure. When her mother had heart trouble, she became the person who managed appointments, coordinated with doctors, handled the calls. When her neighbor's son went through a difficult custody battle, she listened every evening, word for word, crisis for crisis. When her company downsized, she worked twice as hard to prove she was essential.

She did all of this without complaint. She did it with a kind of steady strength that made people lean on her more. She became known as "the one who can handle anything."

What no one saw was the slow erasure of Maria inside all of this.

Her hobbies fell away first. The pottery classes she had loved stopped because there was never time. The novel she had started reading got put down and was never picked up again. Conversations with friends became briefer—always ending with "I should go; there is something I need to handle."

Then the smaller things disappeared: long showers, morning coffee taken slowly, music listened to fully instead of in the background.

She told herself this was temporary. Just until her brother got back on his feet. Just while her mother recovered. Just until work settled down.

But "just until" stretched into years.

By the time Maria was in her mid-forties, she realized she couldn't remember what she liked to do anymore. Not for any purpose, not to impress anyone, not to fix anything—just for the pleasure of doing it. The question "What do *you* want?" had become so unfamiliar that when someone asked it, she had to think for a long time before answering, and even then, she wasn't sure if the answer was genuine or just what she thought she was supposed to say.

One afternoon, Maria sat in her car in a parking lot, waiting for her mother's doctor appointment to finish. She had forty-five minutes of un-planned time—something that rarely happened. She sat in the silence and tried to think of one thing she wanted to do with it.

Nothing came.

She could feel the absence like a physical thing. There was no hobby waiting in the wings. No book she was desperate to return to. No friend she was aching to call just to talk. There was only the thought, "I should probably go back and see if my mother is ready."

Maria put her head on the steering wheel and cried—not dramatically, but with the quiet, exhausted tears of someone who has just realized she forgot to stay alive while she was busy surviving.

That evening, she did something she had not done in years. She sat down at her kitchen table with nothing to do. No purpose, no audience, no problem to solve. Just Maria and forty-five minutes of nothing.

At first, it felt awkward. Her mind kept reaching for things she should be doing. But when she gently put those thoughts down and just sat, some-thing began to surface—not in a rush, but quietly, like a memory rising to the surface of water.

She remembered that she used to paint. Not to be good at it. Not to have anything to show for it. Just because something in her loved the feeling of moving color across paper.

The thought should have remained a memory. But something in her that had been quiet for a very long time spoke up: "What if you did that again?"

The voice was so small she almost missed it.

But she didn't miss it. Instead, she got up, found an old art supply store, and bought watercolors and paper. Not to "restart her hobby" or "get back into art"—phrases that already made it feel like a project, a task, another thing to accomplish.

But simply because her deferred self, the one who had been waiting in the background, had finally asked to be let back in.

The first painting was rough and imperfect. It took her three hours. She showed no one. She posted it nowhere. No one knew or praised or even saw what she had made.

And it was the most restorative thing she had done in seven years.

Over the following months, Maria didn't stop being the person her family counted on. But something shifted. She started to carve out small spaces for the self she had deferred: an hour on Saturday mornings with watercolors, a book she returned to chapter by chapter, a weekly call with an old friend where she actually talked about herself.

These weren't acts of rebellion against her responsibilities. They were acts of remembrance. They said to the part of her that was withering, "You matter too. Your existence is not only in what you do for others."

Her brother noticed the change first. "You seem lighter," he said one day.

"I'm painting again," she told him.

"That's great," he said, and meant it. Then, with a kind of relief that surprised her, he added, "I've been worried about you. You gave so much."

Maria realized something in that moment: the people who loved her didn't need her to disappear in order to feel cared for. They needed her to be present—and you cannot be truly present when you have postponed your own existence.

◆ Questions to Sit With

Where in your life has "surviving" turned into a permanent identity instead of a temporary season?

What have you deferred—about yourself, your interests, your preferences, your presence—in the name of handling what needed to be handled?

If you gave yourself permission to do one small thing this week just because it brings you alive (not because it's productive, not because it helps anyone else, but simply because you want to), what would that be?

What would change in your relationships if the people who depend on you saw you actually living, not just surviving?

How might you become a truer presence to the people you care about if you stopped postponing yourself?

Principle 5 – Staying Where You Can Stay True

Not all relationships are meant to hold you. Some relationships require you to become smaller in order to keep the peace. Some require you to edit yourself, dim your light, apologize for your needs, or pretend that your feelings do not matter as much as the comfort of the other person.

This principle is about learning to distinguish between relationships that help you become more yourself and relationships that ask you to become less.

It is not about being selfish or abandoning people who need you. It is about recognizing that you cannot actually love anyone fully while disappearing from yourself.

◆ Relationships That Shrink You vs. Those That Hold You

A shrinking relationship is one where you feel the need to edit yourself constantly. You monitor what you say, how you express emotion, what you ask for. You anticipate criticism and soften yourself in advance. You leave conversations feeling more exhausted than connected, not because of conflict, but because of the constant work of holding yourself in.

A holding relationship is one where you can be increasingly more yourself—not perfectly, not without friction, but truthfully. You can say something awkward without it becoming a referendum on your worthiness. You can ask for something without fear of punishment or guilt. You can disagree without it meaning you do not belong.

The difference is not always obvious at first. Many shrinking relationships feel safe because they are predictable. You know exactly what will make the other person withdraw, criticize, or hurt, so you learn to avoid those things. This can look like intimacy when it is actually a very careful dance of avoidance.

A holding relationship, on the other hand, can sometimes feel less safe because you are not controlling the outcome. You are risking being fully seen. But that risk is what makes genuine connection possible.

◆ The Cost of Disappearing to Stay Connected

There is a particular kind of loneliness that happens inside relationships. You are physically present, but you are not actually there. You are talking, but you are not saying what you truly think. You are holding hands, but you are holding back your hand.

Over time, this kind of disappearing within connection becomes unbearable. You feel unseen, unheard, unmet. And because the relationship looks fine on the surface—no drama, no clear betrayal—you blame yourself. "There must be something wrong with me that I cannot be satisfied."

But the truth is simpler: you cannot feel truly connected to someone while you are disappearing from yourself.

The principle here is not to leave every difficult relationship. It is to notice which relationships are asking you to shrink, and to make a choice: Can I stay true to myself here? And if the answer is no, what needs to change—or do I need to let this relationship change too?

📖 Tale vignette – She Came Back

For fifteen years, Elena had trained herself to become invisible in her marriage in very specific ways.

She had learned not to talk too much about her own day, because her husband would listen with half his attention and she would feel foolish for taking up space. She had learned to make decisions quietly—what to cook, where to go, how to spend free time—and present them as his ideas so he would feel in control. She had learned to apologize for her sadness, her frustration, her occasional anger, as if her difficult emotions were a personal failing rather than a normal part of being human.

She had learned all of this slowly, without ever making the conscious decision to disappear. It happened in a thousand tiny moments—a comment that stung, an eye roll, a withdrawal of affection that lasted until she apologized for having feelings. Over time, she had shaped herself into the kind of woman he seemed to want: agreeable, steady, never too much.

The strangest part was that she had convinced herself she loved him. And perhaps some version of that was true. But what was also true was that she was suffocating.

The breaking point came not as a dramatic moment, but as a quiet one.

Elena was at lunch with a friend she hadn't seen in years. Over coffee, the friend asked her a simple question: "What are you excited about these days?"

Elena opened her mouth to answer and realized she didn't know. Not because she didn't have excitement—she did, in small private moments, about things she never told anyone. But the habit of shrinking was so deep that the answer that came out was, "Oh, nothing much. Just what he's working on lately has been interesting."

The friend looked at her with a kind of sad recognition. "Elena," she said quietly, "where did you go?"

Elena didn't cry. She just felt the question land in a place that had been waiting a long time for someone to ask it. That night, alone in her car before she went home, she finally admitted it: she had disappeared. And the person her husband loved was not really her—it was the smaller version of her that she had learned to perform.

The realization was unbearable. But what came next was worse: the understanding that she could not stay inside a relationship where she had to pretend to be less in order to be loved.

What happened next took courage. She didn't leave immediately. But she started, very carefully, to come back.

She mentioned something she was thinking about—not asking permission, just saying it. She cried about something that hurt and didn't apologize for the tears. She said no to something, gently but clearly, without offering an alternative or an excuse.

Each small act of coming back was met with resistance. Her husband withdrew. He criticized her for being "difficult." He expressed confusion about why she was "changing." The implication was clear: come back to being small, and we'll be fine.

And Elena had to make a choice.

She could return to the comfortable disappearing. The marriage would smooth out. Life would go back to being predictable and safe.

Or she could stay true to the self that had just begun to come back.

She chose the second one.

The marriage didn't survive the choice. Her husband couldn't accept a woman who had opinions, who said no, who required reciprocal attention and respect. What he wanted was not Elena; he wanted the version of Elena who had vanished.

The divorce was painful. But something unexpected happened in the aftermath: Elena realized that the pain of leaving was actually less lonely than the loneliness of staying.

Three years later, Elena was in a relationship with someone who, when she mentioned something she was excited about, asked her genuine questions about it. When she was upset, he didn't withdraw. When she said no, he respected it. When she was difficult, he stayed.

One day, she realized: this is what a holding relationship feels like. This is what it feels like to not having to disappear.

She also realized something else: she didn't miss the old marriage because she was never fully there to miss.

◆ Questions to Sit With

In which of your important relationships do you feel the most like yourself—and in which ones do you find yourself becoming smaller?

What do you edit out of your conversations with the people closest to you?

If you stayed completely true to yourself in a particular relationship, what are you afraid would happen?

What is the cost to you of staying in a relationship where you have to disappear?

Where in your life might you be confusing "keeping the peace" with "being in a holding relationship"?

Principle 6 – Letting Discomfort
Be Your Teacher

There is a particular kind of discomfort that does not mean you are doing something wrong. It is the discomfort of doing something new, of saying something true, of stepping outside the boundaries you have been contained in, of growing into a space that used to feel too large.

This principle is about learning to distinguish between discomfort that warns you away from danger and discomfort that is simply the feeling of expansion.

◆ Awkward Beginnings and Honest Boundaries

When you start living more truly, life becomes less smooth.

You speak up in a meeting and feel the silence afterward. You set a boundary and feel the other person's hurt. You pursue something that matters to you and feel the judgment or confusion from people who think you should be doing something else. You tell the truth about something difficult and feel the vulnerability that comes with being seen.

This discomfort is real. And your first instinct will be to make it stop.

You can make it stop. You can apologize for speaking up, soften the boundary, abandon the pursuit, take back the truth. The discomfort will ease immediately. The relationships will go back to being smooth. Everything will return to normal.

But you will also return to disappearing.

The principle here is this: not all discomfort is a sign that you are doing something wrong. Sometimes discomfort is a sign that you are doing something brave.

◆ The Difference Between Danger and Growth

Danger discomfort is sharp, immediate, and rooted in a real threat to your safety or wellbeing. If someone is angry in a way that becomes abusive, if a situation genuinely threatens your security, if your body is telling you to run—these are moments to listen. Discomfort rooted in real danger is not something to push through; it is something to respect.

But growth discomfort is different. It is the awkward feeling of doing something for the first time. It is the vulnerability of being honest. It is the strangeness of taking up space where you used to take up less. It is the anxiety that comes from disappointing someone, even if you are doing so gently and for good reasons.

Growth discomfort, when you stay with it, begins to feel less like something is wrong and more like something is changing.

📖 Tale vignette – The Quiet Boundary

For years, Marcus's mother called every evening. The calls were not bad, exactly. She mostly wanted to tell him about her day, ask about his, hear his voice. By all reasonable standards, it was not a burden.

Except it was slowly consuming his evening, every single evening.

He couldn't fully engage with his partner. He couldn't read or think or exist without part of his attention being on the awareness that soon the phone would ring. Even when she didn't call, he found himself thinking about whether she would, checking his phone, feeling a slight guilt that he hoped she was busy.

The call itself was not long—usually twenty minutes. But the mental weight of it, the obligation, the way it carved his evening into "before the call" and "after the call," was significant.

For a long time, Marcus told himself he was being unreasonable. His mother was lonely. She just wanted connection. How could he begrudge her that? Setting a boundary would be selfish and unkind.

But slowly, he began to notice something: he was not actually present during the calls. He was going through the motions while internally resisting. And after the call, instead of feeling connected to his mother, he felt depleted.

One evening, after the call ended, Marcus realized he was angry. Not at his mother, but at himself—for not having the courage to ask for what he needed.

That night, he sat with the discomfort of what he wanted to do. He wanted to suggest that instead of making daily calls, they talk twice a week, on set days, so he could be fully present instead of partially there every night.

The suggestion, he knew, would hurt her. It would feel like rejection. She might cry or say something like, "I guess you do not want to talk to your mother anymore." He would feel guilty. The evening after that conversation would be uncomfortable.

Marcus sat with that discomfort for a long time. It felt cowardly to stay silent just to avoid it. It also felt impossible to speak.

But he had learned something from the people who loved him: sometimes staying true requires moving through discomfort, not around it.

So, he called his mother the next evening.

"I love you," he began, "and I want to be a good son. But I also need to be honest about something. The daily evening calls have become really difficult for me. I find myself dreading them instead of enjoying them, and I think we both deserve better than that. Would you be open to talking twice a week instead, on set days, so that I can be fully present with you?"

The silence that followed was long.

Then his mother said, "I was wondering when you were going to say something."

"You were?" Marcus asked, surprised.

"Yes," she said. "I could feel you pulling away. I didn't want to admit it, so I kept calling, thinking maybe if we just kept doing it, you would stop resisting. But I could tell you weren't really there."

What Marcus had expected to feel—guilt, shame, the weight of hurting her—was tempered by something else: relief. Because his mother, underneath her own neediness, had known. And she had been waiting for him to tell the truth.

The calls became twice a week. In the time that opened up, something unexpected happened: Marcus was actually present during the calls. He actually wanted to talk to his mother. And she, freed from the resentment of constant resistance, was actually able to be herself.

The discomfort Marcus had pushed through—the guilt, the fear of hurting her, the vulnerability of speaking a truth—had been growth discomfort. And on the other side of it was not only a better relationship with his mother, but also the knowledge that he could honor his own needs without abandoning the people he loved.

◆ Questions to Sit With

Where in your life are you experiencing discomfort right now—and is it the discomfort of danger, or the discomfort of growth?

What boundary or honest conversation have you been avoiding because you fear the other person's reaction?

If you moved through that discomfort and spoke the truth anyway, what might become possible?

Who in your life has modeled the ability to feel discomfort and stay true anyway—and what did you see happen on the other side?

What would change if you treated discomfort not as a sign you are doing something wrong, but as a sign you are becoming more yourself?

Principle 7 – Aligning Your Days
With Your Inner Consent

This is the final principle because it is where all the others gather and live.

It is not about achieving some perfect state. It is about the thousands of small moments in a day when you are saying yes or no—to how you spend your time, to what you agree to, to the way you show up, to the words you speak, to the person you become t6hrough small choices.

◆ When Your Actions Finally Match Your Truth

For a long time, your days may have been organized around a script: what you are supposed to do, what earns approval, what is expected. Your actions did not come from your own inner consent. They came from obligation, from fear, from habit, from the weight of other people's needs.

Aligning your days with your inner consent means something very specific: it means that most of the time, your actions come from a place where you are genuinely choosing them, where you understand them, where you can say yes to them as coming from you.

This does not mean everything you do is fun. You will still do dishes, handle frustrations, manage obligations. But the difference is this: you are doing these things because you have chosen to, because you understand why you are doing them, because the choice is yours.

It is the difference between "I have to" and "I choose to, and here's why." And that small shift in language, that tiny shift in ownership, changes everything.

◆ The Power of the Smallest Decisions

The alignment principle lives in the smallest decisions.

Not: "Am I living my best life?" (too big) But: "Right now, am I saying yes because I actually want to, or because I'm afraid to say no?" (small, specific, answerable)

Not: "Have I aligned my life with my values?" (overwhelming) But: "In this conversation, am I being honest, or am I performing?" (observable, in real time)

Not: "Have I finally become the person I'm meant to be?" (impossible) But: "Is this one action aligned with who I'm becoming?" (testable in the moment)

When you pay attention to the smallest decisions, alignment stops being an abstract goal and becomes a practice. It becomes something you can notice, right now, in this moment. It becomes something you can course-correct. It becomes not a destination but a direction.

📖 Tale vignette – The Smallest Decision

On a Tuesday morning, Sarah found herself saying yes to something she didn't want to do.

It was small. A coworker asked if she could cover a meeting while Sarah worked on a deadline that mattered to her. The coworker was pleasant. The request was framed as "only if you are not too busy." Sarah had the space to say no.

But she said yes.

As she was writing the words, "Of course, no problem," Sarah noticed something. She noticed the automatic response, the reflexive accommodation, the moment where her own needs got smaller in order to be agreeable.

By the time she was in the car driving to work, she was frustrated—not with her coworker, but with herself. She had done it again. She had abandoned herself in a micro-moment.

But this time was different. This time, Sarah had been practicing paying attention.

So instead of letting the frustration just sit there, making her resentful and small, she did something she had learned to do: she told the truth.

She texted her coworker. "I need to be honest. When you asked this morning, I said yes because I didn't want to disappoint you. But the truth is I need that meeting time for my deadline, and I'm going to ask for a rain check on covering this one."

Sarah's hands were shaking as she hit send. She was afraid her co-worker would be hurt. She was afraid it would be awkward in the office. She was afraid it would mean something about her—that she was selfish, unhelpful, not a team player.

Her coworker texted back immediately: "Oh thank god. I was actually going to figure something else out anyway. I just didn't want to burden you, but it would have been weird for me to ask. Thanks for being honest."

Sarah sat with that response for a moment. The thing she had been most afraid of—that her honesty would create distance and judgment—hadn't happened. Instead, it had created actually better communication.

And something in her began to shift.

Over the next weeks, Sarah started to notice the pattern. Every time she said yes when she meant no—not because the request was unreasonable, but because she was afraid of the other person's reaction—something inside her shrank a little. And every time she said no gently but clearly, something inside her came back.

It was not dramatic. No one else necessarily noticed. She still showed up, still contributed, still cared about the people around her. But the difference was: she was doing it because she was choosing to, not because she had lost the capacity to choose.

One afternoon, in a meeting, her boss asked, "Sarah, you have seemed different lately. More present. What's changed?"

Sarah paused, then told the truth: "I've been paying attention to the small moments where I'm saying yes because I'm afraid. And I'm starting to say no instead."

"And that's made you more present?" her boss asked.

"Yeah," Sarah said. "Because I'm not half here, half gone, fighting something I agreed to. I'm actually here."

By the end of that conversation, Sarah's boss asked her to lead a new project—something that required her to actually show up fully. "I need someone who is fully in," he said. "And that's you."

It was a strange gift: when Sarah started saying no to the things that didn't align with her inner consent, she ended up being asked to do things that actually mattered.

But more important than the external shift was the internal one. Sarah realized that alignment was not something that happened once, at some future date when she finally had her life figured out. Alignment was something that happened thousands of times a day, in the smallest decisions.

Every time she chose to be honest instead of agreeable. Every time she said yes when she meant yes, instead of when she meant no. Every time she noticed herself disappearing and chose to stay present instead.

These were not big, dramatic changes. They were the smallest decisions. But when you make them again and again, when you practice aligning your actions with your actual consent, something becomes possible: you start to trust yourself. And when you trust yourself, you finally have permission to live as yourself.

◆ Questions to Sit With

Notice one moment today where you said yes when you actually meant no. What were you afraid would happen if you said no?

What is one small decision you could make today that would feel like an alignment—like you choosing yourself instead of disappearing yourself?

How often do you experience your day as something you are choosing versus something that is happening to you?

If you trusted that your inner consent mattered as much as everyone else's expectations, how would you make decisions differently?

What would become possible if you treated the smallest decisions as just as important as the big ones—because they actually are the big ones?

SEVEN PRINCIPLES - Closing Reflection

These seven principles are not a checklist to master, but a practice to return to. They meet you in ordinary moments—when no one is watching, when the choice feels small, and when it would be easier to act on habit instead of intention. Living on purpose isn't about perfection or certainty; it's about awareness. Each time you pause, choose, and align your actions with what truly matters, you bring these principles to life. Over time, those small, conscious choices don't just shape your days—they shape who you become.

Chapter Five

LIVING AS THE AUTHOR OF YOUR LIFE

Returning to the One You Never Stopped Being

There is a moment, sometimes quiet and sometimes sharp, when you realize something that changes everything: you have not been trying to become someone new. You have been trying to remember someone you already were.

◆ You Were Never Broken, Only Interrupted

The person you think you lost—the one who laughed without calculating the cost, who wanted things without apologizing for wanting them, who could say no without explaining, who trusted their own instincts even when no one else understood—that person did not disappear. They were interrupted.

Interrupted by circumstances that demanded you become practical before you became whole.

Interrupted by loss that required you to be strong before you were ready.

Interrupted by obligations that taught you to take up less space so others could take up more.

Interrupted by a thousand small moments when your own needs came last, and staying silent felt like the price of belonging.

The interruption was not malicious. Much of it was necessary. Some of it saved you. But over time, the interruption became so familiar that you forgot it was an interruption at all. You began to believe that the smaller, quieter, more careful version of you was the only version that was ever real.

This chapter is about understanding something essential: **you have not been broken. You have only been on pause.**

And pauses, unlike breaks, can be resumed.

◆ The Architecture of Interruption

When you look back, the interruptions rarely arrive as dramatic moments. They accumulate like weather—gradually, quietly, until the landscape has completely shifted and you are not quite sure when it changed.

You learn early that some feelings are acceptable and some are not. Your sadness is too much; your anger is inconvenient; your joy is inappropriate to the moment. So, you learn to edit yourself in real time, becoming fluent in the language of what is allowed. This is not weakness. This is intelligence. You are learning to survive in the family system you were born into.

Then adolescence arrives with its own form of interruption: the need to belong becomes more urgent than the need to be yourself. You watch what makes people popular, what makes them invisible, what makes them target. You adjust. You perform. You become someone who fits—which often means someone who fits less and less with who you actually are. But the trade feels necessary. Belonging, after all, matters more than almost anything.

Then comes work, or partnership, or parenthood, or loss—and the interruptions deepen. Someone needs you to be strong, so you learn not to cry. Someone needs you to be flexible, so you stop asking for what you need. Someone needs you to be fine, so you become very good at pretending. Each interruption feels temporary. Each one, you tell yourself, is just for now.

But "just for now" stretches. And the self that was on pause waits, patient and faithful, for the moment when you remember that the pause was never supposed to be permanent.

◆ What Happens in the Pause

Something strange occurs when you pause a part of yourself for long enough: you begin to believe that pause is your actual shape.

The person who used to create, to take risks, to try things without guaranteeing success—you tell yourself that person was unrealistic. Young. Naive. The version of you that was more direct, that said what you actually thought instead of what was diplomatic—you believe that person was rude. The part of you that trusted your own instincts before consulting everyone else's opinions—you decide that person was selfish.

So, you do not mourn the interruption. You congratulate yourself on outgrowing it.

But underneath the congratulations, something quietly dies. It is not dramatic. You still function. You still accomplish things. You still show up and do what needs to be done. But there is a hollowness in it—a sense that you are running the machinery of your life while not actually being present for it.

The people closest to you may not even notice, because the version you are showing them still looks fine. Still competent. Still reliable. They may not see the cost, because you have learned to hide the cost so well that sometimes you forget it yourself.

But the cost accumulates.

It accumulates in the ache that appears on Sunday evenings when you think about the week ahead. In the envy that rises when you see someone living openly, honestly, without apology. In the way your chest tightens when someone asks, "What do *you* want?" and you realize you do not know anymore. In the slow, creeping sense that you are not living your life so much as managing it.

This is the hidden price of interruption: not that you stop being capable, but that you stop being present. Not that you fail, but that you succeed at things that do not actually matter to you. Not that you are abandoned, but that you abandon yourself, slowly, in the name of being good enough for everyone else.

◆ The Nine Thresholds as Remembering

This is where the nine thresholds you crossed earlier in this book become essential. They were not asking you to change. They were asking you to remember.

When you noticed you were drifting instead of deciding, you were remembering that you once knew how to choose.

When you saw where you quietly disappear, you were remembering what it felt like to be fully present.

When you recognized admiration as delayed choice, you were remembering that the qualities you admired were already, quietly, yours.

When you met the part of you that kept waiting for "later," you were remembering that you had dreams before they became inconvenient.

When you felt the cost of performing instead of living, you were remembering what authenticity felt like.

When you recognized survival had replaced living, you were remembering joy as something more than relief.

When you heard the question that wouldn't go away, you were remembering your own voice.

When your excuses no longer fit, you were remembering that you have always had choices.

When you remembered you could choose yourself, you were remembering the most radical truth: **that your consent matters.**

Each threshold was a moment of recognition. And recognition, by definition, means seeing something again—something you had seen before, but had forgotten you had seen.

◆ The Seven Principles as Practice

If the thresholds are recognition, then the principles are the daily practice of living from that recognition.

Because recognition without practice is just another nice idea. Another moment of insight that feels true at 2 a.m. but fades by morning. Another thing you understand intellectually but do not actually live.

The principles are where understanding becomes embodied. They are the translation of "I see this" into "I do this."

When you learn to see yourself before trying to fix yourself, you stop treating your life as a project and start treating it as a relationship with yourself. This changes everything, because relationships require presence, not productivity.

When you choose values that feel like home, you stop building a life around what looks impressive and start building around what feels true. And when your days are organized around what feels true, something remarkable happens: you stop exhausting yourself trying to be impressive and start energizing yourself by being real.

When you make decisions instead of drifting, you claim back the small power you have always had: the power of choosing, even in limited circumstances. This power does not solve everything, but it changes your relationship to what remains unsolved.

When you let survival give way to living, you do not abandon responsibility—you restore the part of yourself that deserves care. And when you care for yourself the way you have cared for others, your capacity expands in unexpected ways.

When you stay where you can stay true, you are not being selfish—you are protecting the self that was interrupted, the self that is finally trying to resume.

When you let discomfort be your teacher, you stop fleeing from growth and start moving through it with your eyes open.

When you align your days with your inner consent, you are finally answering the most fundamental question: **whose life is this?**

And the answer, if you have been paying attention, is always the same: **it is yours.**

◆ The Gathering: How It All Lives Together

This is the part where the book asks you to integrate. Not to do everything at once, not to master every principle, but to see how they all live together in a single, imperfect, still-becoming life.

You do not cross threshold one and then move on to threshold two, leaving the first behind. Instead, the thresholds deepen over time. You notice you are drifting; you bring yourself back to deciding. Then, weeks later, in a different context, you drift again—but this time you notice it faster. The threshold does not become past tense. It becomes a recurring recognition, each time a little more integrated.

The same is true with principles. You learn to see yourself before fixing yourself; this becomes a practice that deepens. You choose values that feel like home; this reshapes not one decision but hundreds of small ones. Over time, the principles are not things you do. They become ways you are.

And here is what makes this possible: **you do not need to be perfect at any of them.** You only need to practice.

One day, you make a small choice that is yours, fully aligned with what you actually want. You feel the difference. Nothing external changes, but something internal shifts. You are reminded: "I can do that again."

Another day, you notice yourself disappearing in a conversation and pause. You come back. You speak the truth. It is awkward. But you stayed. And that matters.

Another day, someone asks what you want, and you know the answer. You say it. They react in ways that sting. But you said it anyway. And you survived the reaction. And the next time you are asked, it is a tiny bit easier.

These are not victories. They are small resurrections—moments when the part of you that was interrupted finally gets to step forward again, just for a moment. But moments accumulate. And eventually, moments become a life.

◆ The Return Is Not a Reversal

It is important to understand something clearly: returning to the one you never stopped being is not the same as going back.

You are not trying to become twenty again, or carefree again, or someone with the luxury of not knowing what you now know. The interruption changed you. The years in survival mode taught you things. The patience you learned, the resilience you built, the way you became able to carry what needs and carrying—those things are real and valuable and not lost.

The return is not about erasing what you learned. It is about integrating it.

It is about being someone who can be both strong and vulnerable. Both responsible and playful. Both aware of what others need and clear about what you need. Both capable of sacrificing and unwilling to sacrifice yourself.

This is far more complex than either/or. It requires you to hold paradox—to be both the person who had to grow up too fast and the person who is finally allowing herself to grow as she is becoming. To be both the survivor and the one who is now learning to live.

The woman who comes back to herself does not suddenly stop being a good mother. She becomes a mother who is also present to her own life. The man who starts choosing himself does not become irresponsible. He becomes responsible to himself in a way he never allowed before. The person who stops disappearing doesn't become selfish. They become honest, which sometimes looks selfish to people who are used to them being convenient.

But this is the trade that makes everything else possible: some people may be uncomfortable with your return. That is their work, not yours.

◆ What This Looks Like in Practice

So, what does a life that has integrated the thresholds and principles actually look like? Not perfect. Not seamless. Not "fixed."

It looks like someone who sometimes drifts but catches themselves faster.

Someone who sometimes disappears but remembers to come back.

Someone who sometimes postpones but knows it is a choice, not a sentence.

Someone who sometimes performs but gets tired of it and stops.

Someone who sometimes survives but makes space to live, too.

It looks like someone whose days are not controlled by everyone else's expectations but organized around what they can genuinely say yes to.

It looks like someone who can say no without explaining, who can want things without apologizing, who can ask for what they need without feeling ungrateful.

It looks like someone who still cares deeply about the people they love, but who understands that caring does not require self-erasure.

It looks like someone whose life is, imperfectly, increasingly, undeniably theirs.

◆ The Unfinished Nature of Becoming

There is one last thing you need to know before you close this book: becoming is not something you finish.

You do not cross all nine thresholds and then graduate to a life where you never have to cross them again. You do not master all seven principles and then rest in the certainty that you have finally figured it out. The thresholds and principles are not destinations. They are orientations—ways of being that you return to again and again as your life unfolds.

You will notice you are drifting again—but now you know what it looks like, and you know what to do. You will feel yourself disappearing again—but now you have felt yourself return, and you know it is possible. You will postpone yourself again—but now you know that waiting is not the same as lost, and that resumption is always available.

Each return will be slightly different because you will be slightly different. Each threshold crossed, each principle practiced, makes the next one slightly easier to recognize.

This is not failure. This is rhythm. This is the way humans actually change—not through one perfect decision, but through thousands of small ones. Not through dramatic transformation, but through quiet accumulation.

The person you are becoming is not someone entirely new. It is someone very old coming back into focus.

◆ The Permission You Have Been Waiting For

If you have read this far, you may have been waiting for permission. Permission to stop trying so hard to be someone else's version of acceptable. Permission to want things that are only for you. Permission to disappoint people by living honestly. Permission to be imperfect and still valuable. Permission to be yourself.

I cannot give you that permission.

No one can.

But I can tell you something that might matter: **you do not need it.**

The permission was always yours. It lived in you before anyone told you to apologize for existing. It lived in you before you learned that your needs were inconvenient. It lived in you before you were taught to make yourself smaller.

It is still there. Interrupted, perhaps. Quieted, certainly. But not gone.

You have crossed nine thresholds. You have practiced seven principles. You have read the stories of people who decided to come back. Now the question is not whether you have permission.

The question is: what are you going to do with the fact that you always had it?

The answer to that question is not the end of the book.

It is the beginning of your life.

Chapter Six

———— ◆◇◆ ————

BRINGING THE SELF BACK INTO THE ORDINARY DAY

◆ **Work, Love, Time, and Attention From the Inside Out**

T he thresholds you have crossed and the principles you have learned do not live in some future, perfected version of your life. They live in the ordinary moments you are moving through right now.

This chapter is about that translation: how to bring the self you are remembering back into the actual, imperfect, still-demanding life you have today.

Because here is what happens when you finally wake up to your own life: you still have to go to work. You still have to show up in relationships. You still have to manage time, make decisions, handle conflict, answer emails, and keep things functioning. The thresholds and principles do not erase any of that. They simply change the place you are moving from while you are doing it.

This is not a chapter about optimizing your life or achieving some new level of productivity. It is a chapter about presence.

Because presence changes everything—not because it makes everything easier, but because it makes everything yours.

How This Works in Practice

When you bring the self-back to work, your relationship to work changes before anything external necessarily shifts.

You may still have the same job, the same boss, the same frustrations. But if you are making choices from alignment instead of from fear, if you are saying yes when you mean yes and no when you mean no, if you are showing up with presence instead of performance—the experience of the work itself transforms.

You stop being a person who is *at* work and become a person who is *doing* work.

The difference is subtle but complete.

At work, you might:

Notice when you are saying yes out of anxiety instead of genuine availability.

Pause before responding to criticism and choose how to actually respond instead of reacting.

Speak an honest perspective in a meeting, even if it's uncomfortable, because you have learned that your truth matters.

Protect time and energy for what is actually important to you, without explaining or apologizing.

Step back from being the person everyone leans on to fix things, because you have learned that over-functioning is its own kind of disappearing.

None of these require you to quit your job or blow up your career. They require you to stop treating yourself as a machine to be optimized and start treating yourself as a human being who deserves presence in their own workdays.

The same is true in love and partnership.

When you bring the self-back to your relationships, the person you are with encounters someone more real. Not someone who has it all figured out. Not someone who never struggles or disagrees. But someone who is actually there—in the conversation, in the conflict, in the quiet moments, in the difficulty.

You might:

Show up with your actual feelings instead of the version you think will keep the peace.

Ask for what you actually need, knowing that asking might disappoint someone and knowing that is their work, not yours.

Listen not to fix or manage, but to understand—which paradoxically makes you more present and more helpful.

Say no to demands that erode you, even when the person you love feels hurt by it, because you have learned that disappearing is not love.

Stay in conflict instead of smoothing it over, because you have learned that real connection lives on the other side of honest difficulty.

This does not mean your relationships become perfect. It means they become real. And realness, it turns out, is what people actually hunger for beneath all the politeness.

With time and attention, the same principle applies.

Time is not something that happens to you. It is something you are actively deciding how to spend. Every moment you choose to be fully present to what you are actually doing—instead of half-present while worrying about what comes next—is a moment you have taken back.

Attention is the same. Where you place your attention is a choice. Not in some grandiose, meditate-on-a-mountaintop way, but in the small, constant way: Are you present for this conversation, or are you already mentally moved to the next task? Are you tasting this meal, or are you eating while thinking about dinner? Are you hearing what this person is actually saying, or are you already composing your response?

These are not failures. They are places where you get to choose again.

◆ Letting Small Choices Carry Big Truths

The reason presence matters so much is that presence is where choice actually lives.

You cannot choose something you are not paying attention to. You cannot align with your values if you are not present enough to notice where you are misaligned. You cannot stay true to yourself if you are not awake enough to see when you are disappearing.

So, the small choices—the ones that seem insignificant in the moment—carry something enormous.

They carry the truth that you can choose.

When you choose to fully listen in a conversation instead of half-listening while thinking about what to say next, you are telling yourself, "My presence matters. This moment is worth my full attention."

When you choose to say no to something, even though it is inconvenient and will disappoint someone, you are telling yourself, "My capacity has limits, and honoring those limits is not selfish."

When you choose to speak an honest perspective instead of staying silent to avoid conflict, you are telling yourself, "My truth deserves to be heard, even if it makes things awkward."

When you choose to take a walk alone, to create something, to sit with a difficult feeling instead of distracting from it, you are telling yourself, "I deserve care from myself."

When you choose to rest instead of pushing through, to ask for help instead of managing alone, to play instead of only being productive, you are telling yourself, "I am allowed to exist for reasons beyond what I accomplish."

Each small choice is a small resurrection.

And small resurrections, accumulated over time, become a life.

The woman in the bridge story—the one who came back to herself—did not wake up one day with a perfect, fully aligned life. She woke up and chose to listen to her partner. She chose to laugh at something impractical. She chose to protect a small space for herself, even though the house was full. She chose to stay true, even when her children needed time to adjust.

None of those choices were easy. But each one was available to her—not someday, but right then, in the ordinary moment she was in.

That is what this chapter is really about: helping you see that the small choices you have available right now are enough.

You do not need to wait for better circumstances, more confidence, or perfect clarity. You can choose presence today. You can choose honesty today. You can choose yourself, even in small ways, today.

◆ The Ordinary Becomes Sacred When You Are Present to It

There is a strange alchemy that happens when you stop trying to escape your ordinary life and start actually inhabiting it.

The dishes are still dishes. The commute is still a commute. The difficult conversation is still difficult. Nothing magical happens. But something shifts: you stop experiencing these moments as obstacles to real life and start experiencing them as real life itself.

This is the paradox that the thresholds and principles point toward: the life you have been postponing, the person you have been waiting to become, is not somewhere else. It is here. It is available in how you wash the dishes, in how you listen during the commute, and in how you show up in the difficult conversation.

Sacredness does not require candlelight and silence. It requires presence.

When you are fully present for an ordinary conversation with someone you love, it becomes sacred—not because of what is being said, but because you are actually there, fully there, listening without planning, hearing without judgment.

When you are fully present for work that matters to you, even if the work is unglamorous—writing emails, solving problems, creating something that will be used by someone you will never meet—it becomes sacred. Because you are doing it with intention. You chose to be there.

When you are fully present for the small ritual of making coffee, or taking a shower, or walking to your car, these moments are no longer transitions between "real life." They become life itself.

Most people spend their days moving through moments they are not actually present for, waiting for the next thing to finally make them happy, finally make them feel alive, finally make them feel alive, finally make them matter.

But presence does not wait. It is available now.

This does not mean you need to love every moment of your life. Some things are still hard, boring, frustrating. But even in those moments, you can choose to be there fully, to engage with what is actually happening instead of resisting it or escaping it mentally.

And that choice—that simple choice to be present—is what transforms the ordinary into something that feels like it is actually yours.

◆ Building a Life That Includes You

This is what bringing the self-back means in practical terms: it means your own presence, your own needs, your own aliveness become a factor in how you spend your time.

Not the *only* factor. You still care about people, about work, about responsibilities. But you are no longer the last person you consider.

You might:

Schedule time for yourself the way you schedule meetings—not as a luxury, but as a non-negotiable part of how you keep yourself functioning.

Notice your energy throughout the day and adjust what you are doing based on what you actually have to give, instead of running on empty until collapse.

Protect conversations that matter to you, instead of always being available for conversations that serve someone else's needs.

Say no to opportunities that do not align with who you are becoming, even if they look impressive or are what you "should" want.

Invest in the parts of yourself that make you feel alive—creativity, movement, learning, solitude, connection—because those investments make you more present in everything else you do.

These are not acts of rebellion. They are acts of respect—respect for the self that has finally decided to show up.

And when you respect yourself this way, something remarkable happens: you become more available to the people who actually matter to you. Not because you are over-functioning, but because you are not half-gone. Not because you are performing being fine, but because you actually have some resources left over to be genuinely there.

The self you are bringing back into your ordinary life is not a luxury addition. It is the foundation that makes everything else sustainable.

◆ When You Slip Back Into Absence

It is important to know: you will slip.

You will have days, weeks, sometimes longer stretches where you fall back into old patterns. Where you over-commit and disappear. Where you perform and forget to be present. Where you put yourself last and call it being responsible.

This is not failure.

This is the rhythm of becoming. You are not meant to get it right and stay there. You are meant to notice when you have slipped and chosen again.

The difference between now and before is this: now you will notice. You will feel the hollowness of being absent from your own life. You will recognize the familiar feeling of disappearing. And you will know that you can turn back toward yourself.

Because you have done it before. You know it is possible.

The ordinary moments will still be there. The small choices will still be available. And every time you choose presence over absence, every time you choose your own honesty over someone else's comfort, every time you choose yourself even in a small way, you are affirming: "This life is mine. And I am finally going to live it."

That is what it looks like to bring the self-back into your ordinary day.

Chapter Seven

WHEN YOU FORGET
AND REMEMBER
AGAIN

◆ Slipping Back Into Roles Without Shame

You will forget. You will have a conversation and realize, hours later, that you performed the entire thing. You will say yes to something you meant to say no to. You will catch yourself disappearing in a relationship you thought you had finally become honest in. You will notice that you have fallen back into survival mode, optimizing and managing and forgetting to actually live.

And your first instinct will be to shame yourself.

I thought I had worked through this. I should know better by now. Why do I keep doing this? What is wrong with me that I cannot seem to stay awake?

This is the moment to pause.

Because what is happening is not failure. It is rhythm. It is the way humans actually change—not through one perfect decision, but through thousands of small ones. Not through dramatic transformation, but through the patient accumulation of moments where you notice and choose again.

The roles you slip back into are old, familiar, deeply grooved. They kept you safe once. They taught you how to survive in systems that demanded you be less than yourself. Of course they are still there. Of course, you still reach for them sometimes, especially when you are tired, scared, or under pressure.

Slipping back does not erase what you have learned. It does not mean you were never awake. It means you are human—and humans are not meant to be perfect; they are meant to be honest about their imperfection and keep trying anyway.

Here is what matters: Can you notice when you have slipped? And can you choose differently the next time?

If the answer is yes, then you are still on the path. You are still becoming.

How to Notice Without Judgment

The key to slipping back without staying stuck is learning to notice without shame.

Shame says: Look at what you did. You are the problem.

Honesty says: Look at what you did. What was happening in you that made that choice seem necessary?

The difference is everything.

When you slip back into a familiar role, pause and ask:

What was I afraid of? (Afraid of disappointing someone? Of conflict? Of not being enough?)

What did I need in that moment? (Did I need rest? Did I need to be taken seriously? Did I need reassurance?)

Why did the old pattern feel safer than the new one? (Because it is familiar. Because it has always worked before. Because trying something new is harder than going back to what I know.)

These are not excuses. They are explanations. And explanations give you information you can actually work with.

If you slipped back into people-pleasing because you were exhausted, then what you need is rest, not self-condemnation. If you disappeared in a conversation because you were afraid of conflict, then what you need is practice with discomfort, not shame. If you said yes to something you didn't want because you feared disappointing someone, then what you need is to tolerate the discomfort of that disappointment, not to punish yourself.

Once you understand what made the slip happen, you are no longer powerless. You have information. And information is where choice lives.

◆ Beginning Again Without Starting Over

The most important thing to know about slipping back is this: **you do not have to start over.**

Starting over implies that all your progress is erased, that you are back at the beginning, that everything you learned is lost. That is not true.

You are not starting over. You are beginning again.

Beginning again means:

You remember what you learned about yourself.

You know what it feels like to be honest.

You have felt yourself return, so you know it is possible.

You have seen what happens when you choose yourself, even in small ways.

You have proof that the life you want is not theoretical; it is available to you.

All of that is still true, even in the moment you slip.

So, when you notice you have disappeared again, you do not need to:

Go back and re-read everything.

Start a new program or try a new strategy.

Convince yourself that you can change because you already know you can.

Begin from a place of "I am broken and need to be fixed."

What you need to do is simpler:

Notice. Understand. Choose again.

That is all.

The next time you are in a similar situation, you might still slip. That is okay. You are learning a new way of being, and new ways take time to root. But each time you notice and choose again, the gap between the slip and the awareness gets smaller. The slip becomes less automatic and more intentional.

This is the spiral, not the line.

◆ The Spiral, Not the Line

We are taught to think of progress as a line.

You start here. You move forward. You arrive at the destination, and you are done. Everything behind you is behind you. You do not go back.

But that is not how change works.

Real change is a spiral. You move through the same themes again and again—the same fears, the same patterns, the same choices, but each time you come around, you are at a slightly different altitude. You see more clearly. You understand more deeply. You are able to choose from a slightly more expanded place.

You might visit the threshold of "disappearing" three times in your life. The first time, you might not even recognize it as disappearing; you just feel numb. The second time, you notice but feel powerless to change it. The third time, you recognize it happening and are able to course-correct midway through. The fourth time—years later, in a new relationship or new context—you might prevent it from happening in the first place.

You are not failing by visiting the same threshold twice. You are spiraling deeper into understanding it.

The same is true with principles. You might practice "seeing before striving" and feel like you finally get it. Then months later, you are in a stressful situation, and you find yourself back in self-attack mode, trying to force yourself to change. You have not lost the principle. You have just discovered another layer of where you use self-attack—a place you were not ready to see before.

This spiral is not a failure of the journey. It is the journey itself.

And the beautiful part is each time you spiral back to something you thought you had resolved, you are not starting from zero. You are starting from a place of greater awareness. You are closer to the center than you were the last time. And your capacity to respond with compassion instead of judgment has deepened.

The spiral means you are not trying to transcend your humanness. You are trying to integrate it—to become someone who is honest about their patterns, patient with their learning, and willing to choose again and again.

◆ What This Looks Like in Practice

In practice, slipping and spiraling looks like this:

You have a difficult conversation with someone you love. Afterward, you realize you performed the whole thing—you softened your needs, you smoothed over conflict, you prioritized their comfort over your honesty. For a moment, you feel the shame: *I should have known better.*

But then you remember: you have done this before. And you know what to do.

You sit with it. You understand: you were afraid that honesty would hurt them or make them angry or cause them to withdraw. And that fear felt real enough to make the old pattern seem necessary.

Then you make a choice: tomorrow, or next week, you will go back and have the conversation again. Not perfectly. But honestly. You will say what you actually meant to say. You will let them feel whatever they feel. You will sit with discomfort.

And when you do, something shifts. Not because the conversation goes perfectly—it might not. But because you did not abandon yourself. You came back.

This is not a grand transformation. It is a small resurrection.

And small resurrections, accumulated over time, become life.

Chapter Eight

WHEN THE PEOPLE AROUND YOU DO NOT UNDERSTAND

The Unexpected Resistance

Y ou have crossed the thresholds. You have begun to practice the principles. You are making different choices. You are saying no when you used to say yes. You are speaking truth when you used to stay silent. You are protecting time for yourself when you used to give it all away.

And the people around you are not happy about it.

This is the chapter no one tells you about when they talk about personal transformation. They talk about how liberating it will feel. How much lighter you will be. How much better your relationships will become once you are being authentic.

But they do not talk about the resistance.

Your mother calls and you do not answer immediately. She leaves a message: "I guess you are too busy for your family now." Your partner wants you to be available for something and you say you need time for yourself. They say: "You are being selfish." Your best friend asks you to do something you no longer want to do and you say no. They say: "You have changed. You are not the person I thought you were."

And your children look at you with confusion when you say you need to rest instead of playing. They ask why you are not available the way you used to be. They resist the new boundaries with the particular intensity that only children can muster.

And suddenly, your transformation—which felt so necessary, so honest, so right—starts to feel like betrayal, especially to them.

This chapter is about that moment: what happens when the people around you resist your change, and most painfully, when your children are the ones who do not understand. It is about how to hold your ground without becoming rigid, defensive, or cruel—while also honoring the real needs of the people who depend on you.

◆ Why People Resist Your Change

The people around you have gotten used to you a certain way. They have built their own systems around how you are. Your mother has organized her emotional life around the fact that you will always be there for her. Your partner has organized their life around the fact that you will accommodate their needs. Your friends have organized their friendships around the version of you that always shows up, always listens, always puts their needs first.

Your children have also learned you in a particular way: as the parent who is endlessly available, endlessly patient, endlessly present, often at the expense of yourself.

When you change, you are not just changing yourself. You are changing the contract everyone has with you.

And people do not like that.

Not because they are bad people, but because stability—even unhealthy stability—feels safe. When you disrupt that stability, people feel threatened.

Your mother might feel: "If you are not always available, I cannot depend on you the way I thought I could. I am more alone than I realized."

Your partner might feel: "If you are prioritizing yourself, I am no longer your priority. Our relationship is changing in ways I did not choose."

Your friends might feel: "If you are setting boundaries with me, I am being judged. Our friendship is not what I thought it was."

Your children might feel: "My parent used to be always available. Now they are not. Something changed and I do not know what it means, and I do not like it."

None of these feelings are rational exactly. But they are human. And they are real. People resist change in others because change in others forces change in themselves. And change is threatening.

◆ The Psychology of Projection and Blame

When someone resists your change, they often make your change about them.

They say things like: "You have become cold." What they mean is: "I feel the distance created by your new boundaries, and it makes me uncomfortable."

They say: "You are being selfish now." What they mean is: "You used to serve me, and now you are serving yourself, and that feels like rejection."

They say: "You are not the person I fell in love with." What they mean is: "I built my life around a version of you that no longer exists, and I do not know how to rebuild."

Your children may say: "You do not love me as much as you used to. You are mean now. Why do you not want to spend time with me? You are never here anymore. You care about yourself more than you care about me." These statements are not true, but they feel true to your child because something has changed and they are scared.

Instead of naming their fear or grief, people blame you. They suggest that *you* are the problem—that you have become worse, harder, colder, more selfish.

If you are not careful, you start to believe them. You question yourself, soften your boundaries, go back to people-pleasing, begin performing again—just to make others more comfortable.

◆ The Particular Ache of Your Children's Resistance

Your children did not choose this relationship; they were born into it. They depend on you, and they have grown up inside the version of you who once had no boundaries. From their perspective, everything was working fine: you were there, you took care of them, that was the deal.

When you change the deal, they did not consent to that change. Your eight-year-old does not understand that you have postponed yourself for years. Your teenager does not understand that you are claiming a life beyond parenting. Your adult child may understand intellectually, but emotionally they are grieving the parent who would always drop everything.

Their grief is real. Your need to change is real. Both are true at the same time. The work is to honor both truths without abandoning yourself again.

Children resist change differently by age:

- Young children often become clingy, melt down, regress, or test boundaries harder. Behavior says: "Something changed. I do not know what or why. I am scared."

- Teenagers may say, "You have changed. You are not the parent I thought you were," withdraw emotionally, or weaponize your new boundaries as proof you do not care. Underneath is fear that they are no longer your priority.

- Adult children may make subtle comments, test whether your boundaries are real, or express hurt that you are not endlessly available. They are grieving the familiar—even if it was unhealthy.

◆ Why Your Change Feels Like Betrayal

When you have been meeting someone else's needs at the expense of your own, you have been sending a clear message: "Your needs matter more than mine. Your comfort is more important than my authenticity. Your happiness is my responsibility."

People build their relationship with you around that message. So when you start saying no, setting boundaries, and prioritizing yourself, you are not just changing behaviors—you are changing the message.

You are now saying: "Your needs do not matter more than mine. Your comfort is not my responsibility. I was wrong to send that message, and I am changing it now."

Those who benefited from the old message feel hurt. It feels like you are taking away something that was promised: unlimited access to you, your time, your energy, your emotional labor.

To them, that feels like betrayal, even if to you it feels like the first honest step back toward yourself.

◆ The Guilt of Being "Selfish" With the People You Love

You will likely feel guilt everywhere, but it is sharpest with your children.

You have been told that good parents put their children first, always. To put yourself anywhere but last can feel like violating that oath. You think: "How can I possibly choose myself when they depend on me?"

The hard truth is that you cannot put your children first 100% of the time without eventually disappearing. Disappeared parents are exhausted, resentful, numb—and children feel that, even if you never say it.

The best thing you can do for your children is take care of yourself *alongside* taking care of them. Otherwise, you are teaching them that love equals self-erasure—and they will either repeat that pattern or demand it from others.

The same is true for partners, parents, and friends: guilt can be used—consciously or not—to pull you back into sacrifice. Phrases like "If you cared, you would be here," or "After everything I've done..." rest on a false premise that love requires self-abandonment. Healthy love requires boundaries.

Your guilt is evidence that you care, not evidence that you are wrong. Caring that is sustainable must include you.

◆ Holding Your Ground Without Becoming Rigid

The challenge is to hold your boundaries while holding compassion. This is the difference between a boundary and a punishment.

Holding your ground means:

Not re-explaining your boundary every time someone objects; they heard you.

Not softening your boundary just to relieve someone else's discomfort.

Not taking resistance personally; it is about their adaptation, not your worth.

Not defending your choices as if you are on trial.

Accepting that some people will not like your change—and that this is their work.

Holding your ground does *not* mean:

Becoming cold or cruel.

Cutting people off abruptly when change could be gradual.

Using boundaries to punish or prove something.

Withdrawing love.

Refusing to listen to legitimate concerns.

If you notice yourself getting rigid or self-righteous, that is information: you may be slipping into punishment. But if the boundary is true and necessary, and you can hold it with clarity and kindness, you are doing the work.

◆ How to Hold Your Boundaries as a Parent

As a parent, you are walking a narrower ledge: you must still care for real, non-negotiable needs while also protecting your own.

Practically, this looks like:

Being honest about your needs without making them your child's fault: "I need some time alone for an hour. Then we can do something together."

Not disappearing but not abandoning yourself: "I can listen for fifteen minutes, and then I need to rest."

Acknowledging their pain without collapsing under it: "I know you are sad I need quiet time. It is okay to be sad. And I still need this."

Staying consistent when they test the boundary; consistency teaches that boundaries are real.

Repairing when you do not get it right: "I was short with you, and that was not okay. I was frustrated with myself, not you. I am sorry."

If they are young, you structure support—other caregivers, clear "on/off" times, including them in some of your self-care—so their real needs are met while you also exist as a human being, not a utility.

Over time, they learn that people have limits, that boundaries are normal, and that love and self-respect can coexist.

📖 Tale vignette - The Mother Who Came Back to Herself

For fifteen years, Sarah organized her entire life around her three children. She woke early to cook, rearranged her schedule for every need, sat through every game and event. She had no boundaries and no independent life. She called it love and good motherhood. Underneath, she was drowning.

When her youngest turned fourteen, something shifted. She realized she had nothing left of herself. She went to therapy, began setting boundaries, and started protecting time for herself. Her children noticed immediately.

"Why are you always working on yourself now?" her youngest asked.

"You seem different. Not as fun. Kind of distant," said the middle one

"Are you okay? You seem weird," her oldest said.

The guilt was crushing. She considered going back. But she knew that would mean disappearing again.

Instead, she sat each child down. To the youngest: "I know I am different. I am taking better care of myself, so I am not always available like before. That does not mean I love you less. It means I am learning to love myself, and I want you to learn that too."

To the middle child: "I know I am not as 'fun' all the time. I am tired sometimes now. I am setting boundaries instead of always saying yes. It might make me less fun, but it makes me more real. I think that is better."

To the oldest: "I am actually more okay than I have been. I am finally taking care of myself. That changes things between us. You cannot lean on me in the same way, but I am still here—just differently."

Over months, things have shifted. Her youngest began to notice her mother was happier and more present when she *was* there. Her middle child felt closer because the relationship was less performative. Her oldest started his own work of figuring out who he was beyond others' expectations.

Sarah still showed up, still loved them fiercely—but from a place where she also existed. She was no longer just surviving motherhood; she was parenting as a person who also had a life.

◆ The Long Game

You will not set a boundary and see instant harmony. You will set a boundary and watch people resist, withdraw, test, and doubt. Your children will protest. Your family may sulk or lash out. Your friends may pull away.

Your task is to stay with discomfort without reverting to the old pattern. To tolerate their temporary unhappiness so you do not return to your permanent self-abandonment.

Over weeks, months, and years, some people will adjust. Some relationships will deepen because they are finally honest. Some will fade because they depended on your disappearance to function. All of this is data about what was real and what was only ever built on your self-erasure.

◆ Questions to Sit With

Who in your life is resisting your change most strongly—and what exactly are they resisting?

How are your children specifically reacting? What are they saying or showing you?

What guilt are you carrying about their discomfort, and is it being used—by you or them—to pull you back?

Can you hold your boundary while validating their experience? What would that sound like in a single sentence?

Are you explaining your change in age-appropriate ways, especially to your kids, so they know this is not about loving them less?

Where do you see even small signs that people are adjusting to the new you?

Which relationships might not survive your change—and can you grieve that while still refusing to abandon yourself again?

◆ A Final Word: The Relationships That Deepen

It is worth knowing that not all relationships deteriorate when you change. Some actually deepen.

The people who love you for who you actually are—not who you are for them, but who you are as a person—will eventually understand. They may struggle at first. But they will come around.

Because the truth is: when you stop disappearing, when you stop performing, when you start being authentic—you actually become easier to love. Because people get to love the real you, not the version of you that you have been performing.

And that is worth the temporary discomfort.

That is worth holding your ground.

PART V
CONTINUATION

Staying in a Relationship with Yourself

There is no finish line.

    What matters is not what you realized once,

    but how you listen to moving forward.

    This final part is not an ending.

    It is a handoff—

    from these pages
    back to your life.

Chapter Nine

SET OF TOOLS FOR SELF-REALIZATION

Ways of Noticing Without Turning Yourself into a Project

This part of his book is not asking you to fix yourself.

It is asking you to see yourself more clearly—and then to live from what you see.

The tools that follow are not techniques for improvement. They are not habits to optimize or practice to master. They are simple ways of paying attention that help you hear what you have been overriding.

You do not need to use all of them. You do not need to use any of them perfectly. One tool used honestly is more powerful than many tools used performatively.

Think of these as lenses, not instructions.

1. Journaling as Noticing (Not Performing)

Journaling is useful only when it tells you something you didn't already approve of.

This is not about recording your day or narrating your thoughts in polished language. It is about letting what is unfinished, inconvenient, or unflattering come into view.

Try writing without rereading.

Stop mid-sentence when your time is up.

Do not correct yourself.

Useful questions include:

What did I not say today that wanted to be said?

Where did I agree outwardly while resisting inwardly?

What truth keeps repeating, even when I try to outgrow it?

If journaling makes you feel virtuous but unchanged, it has turned into performance.

2. Reflection (Used as a Doorway, Not a Home)

Reflection is the space between experience and response.

Used well, it clarifies.

Used poorly, it becomes a loop.

Reflection becomes unhelpful when it replaces movement—when understanding your life becomes a substitute for living it.

A simple way to reflect without getting stuck:

What happened?

What did I feel before I explained it?

What story did I tell myself about that feeling?

Then stop.

If reflection leaves you clearer, it is working. If it leaves you heavier, it has turned into avoidance.

Reflection is meant to open a door, not become the room you live in.

3. The Body as an Honest Witness

Your body registers truth before your mind organizes a defense.

Pay attention to:

where tension appears when you say yes

where fatigue shows up after certain conversations

where energy returns, even when something is difficult

After interactions, quietly ask:

Do I feel expanded or contracted?

Did I override something to keep things smooth?

Your body is not dramatic.

It is precise.

When the body consistently resists what the mind keeps justifying, listen.

4. Envy as Information

Quiet envy is often a message, not a flaw.

It does not mean you want someone else's life.

It means something in you recognizes itself.

When envy appears, ask:

What quality or freedom am I responding to?

What does this reveal about what I want but have postponed?

Envy points toward unlived parts of you.

Handled gently, it becomes guidance.

5. Language Audits

Notice the phrases you repeat automatically:

"I do not really have a choice."

"It's just the way it is."

"I should be grateful."

"Maybe later."

These phrases often signal unexamined consent.

You may not be trapped.

You may be choosing—without acknowledging the cost.

Self-realization begins when you hear your own language clearly.

6. Role Fatigue

List the roles you are good at:

the responsible one

the achiever

the caretaker

the steady one

the peacemaker

Then ask:

Who am I when I'm not performing this role?

What would I fear losing if I stopped excelling at it?

Fatigue is often the body's way of saying:

This role is no longer big enough for me.

7. Micro-Experiments

Self-realization deepens through contact, not certainty.

Instead of big changes, try small, reversible acts:

twenty minutes a week with something you once loved

one honest nowhere you would normally default to yes

doing something imperfectly without explaining yourself

The question is not:

Did this change my life?

The question is:

Did I feel more like myself?

8. Listening to Resistance

Resistance is rarely laziness.

It is usually protecting:

belonging

stability

identity

safety

Instead of pushing through it, ask:

What would this cost me socially or emotionally?

What am I afraid of losing if I change?

Resistance carries information.

Treat it as a signal, not an enemy.

9. One Question, Held Over Time

Choose one honest question and let it follow you:

Where am I living smaller than I need to?

What part of me keeps waiting for permission?

What do I already know but have not honored?

Do not rush to answer it.

Some questions do their work quietly, in the background of ordinary days.

A Final Word About Tools

None of these tools will change your life on their own.

What changes a life is not insight, reflection, or even courage.

What changes a life is honoring what you already know—in small, consistent ways—until your outer life begins to match your inner consent.

You do not need to become someone new.

You need to stop abandoning the person who is already here.

These tools are simply ways of remembering how to listen.

Closing Reflection

THE THRESHOLD OF DECISIONS

T ales of the self are, at their core, tales of decisions. Every threshold you have crossed in these pages has brought you to one: stay on the familiar path of drifting, disappearing, postponing, performing, surviving, excusing—or choose, in some small but decisive way, to remember yourself.

The details are different from life to life, but the pattern is strangely consistent. The moments that change a life rarely arrive with fanfare; they arrive as a scene you cannot forget, a sentence you cannot ignore, or a glimpse of your life that suddenly feels unbearable to sleepwalk through.

The night the lights came on

A man drives home along a dark two-lane road he has taken a thousand times—same gas station, same faded billboard, same left turn. The route is muscle memory. Most nights, he does it with his attention closed.

Tonight, something small breaks the spell. A truck swerves over the line, headlights sweeping across the trees. For a moment, he realizes just how narrow the line is between an ordinary night and when everything changes. His heart pounds. In that flash, the road he has treated as harmless routine reveals itself as what it has always been: a place where his presence matters.

He pulls into his driveway a different man. Nothing dramatic has happened. No accident, no sirens. But something in him has crossed a line. Tomorrow, he will stop working at midnight. Next week, he will book the appointment he has delayed for years. Months from now, he will barely remember the truck, but he will be living a life that started to change with that moment.

Stories like this—and books such as *The Celestine Prophecy*—explore the moment when ordinary life becomes infused with deeper awareness. The road did not change. His way of moving through it did. That is what these thresholds have been preparing you for: not a new universe, but a new way of inhabiting the one you already have.

The café, the mirror, and recognition

You met Daniel in the café for the same reason you met that driver on the road: to see your own life from the outside long enough to recognize it.

Daniel's crisis is not that his life is uniquely tragic. His crisis is that it is vaguely fine—fine enough to postpone change, not fine enough to feel alive. He comes to the same table, orders the same drink, watches the same man in the blue shirt across the aisle. At first it is admiration: *That guy looks like the kind of person who actually lives.* Calm. Present. Unhurried.

For a while, watching is enough. It feels like progress just to study someone who seems to have what he lacks. But slowly, something shifts. The reflection in the clouded mirror behind his booth starts to behave strangely. The man in the blue shirt appears where Daniel sits. The jacket is his. The tiredness in the eyes is his.

One morning, the man speaks to him: "You do not admire me. You recognize me."

The story is not about magic. It is about ownership. The café has not changed. The mirror does not change. What changes is the answer to a single question: *Whose life is this, really?* As soon as Daniel admits that the reflection is not a stranger but a possibility, he cannot go back to being just an observer.

Stories like this work because they sneak past your defenses. They do not lecture you about free will. They simply bring you to a scene where someone like you can no longer hide from the fact that continuing as you are is also a decision.

The cost of staying on autopilot

The danger is not that you will never have a big, cinematic crossroads. The danger is that you will explain away the smaller ones until your life quietly hardens around them.

You tell yourself you are "still thinking about it" while the window quietly closes. You say, "This is not the right time," so many times that "never" moves in and makes itself at home. You treat admiration—of fit people, honest people, courageous people, creative people—as a substitute for the choices that would make you one of them.

At some point, this stops being ignorance and becomes a form of self-betrayal. Every time you see clearly and then deliberately look away, you teach yourself a story: *I am the kind of person who notices the truth and does nothing about it.* The longer you live inside that story, the harder it becomes to imagine anything else.

The thresholds in this book have been interrupting that story. They have named the places where you drift, disappear, postpone, perform, survive, excuse, and, finally, remember. They have shown you that awareness without action is its own kind of autopilot—quieter than denial, but just as effective at keeping your life exactly the same.

When insight is no longer enough

Many people live in a strange half-light: over-educated and under-changed. They can explain their patterns with impressive nuance. They know their attachment style, their enneagram number, their trauma history, their love language. They can map out, in exquisite detail, why they do what they do—and still go home to the exact same arguments, the exact same late-night scrolling, the exact same life they say they long to leave.

Insight without decision becomes a comfortable prison. It lets you feel sophisticated about your stuckness. It gives you language without movement, explanation without risk. Eventually, the story of *why* you are this way starts to matter more to you than the question of whether you must *stay* this way.

The tales in this book have not been asking you to analyze them. They have been asking: *Where, in your own life, does this scene rhyme?* When you feel that uncomfortable echo—when Daniel's mirror feels too familiar, when the driver's narrow escape feels like your own near-miss—that is the moment when the story hands the pen back to you.

Two kinds of decisions

There are decisions that decorate your life and decisions that re-route it.

Decorating decisions sound like this:

"I'm going to buy a new planner."

"I'm going to follow five more inspiring accounts."

"I'm going to sign up for the gym and see what happens."

They change your environment, your tools, your inputs. They are not bad—but left alone, they rarely move the story.

Re-routing decisions sound quieter, but they cut deeper:

"I am going to stop telling myself I do not have a choice here."

"I am going to end this thing that is killing me, even though I do not know what comes next."

"I am going to pick one small, measurable commitment and honor it as if my life depends on it—because, in the long run, it does."

These are the decisions that bend a timeline. They do not need fanfare. They need follow-through.

You are already writing the next chapter

It is tempting to imagine that your "big decision" is somewhere out there—a future moment when the sky opens, your purpose arrives fully formed, and you finally become the person you were meant to be.

If these tales have done their work, that illusion should be harder to cling to now.

You are already making the decisions that will shape your life:

Every time you ignore the quiet dread that rises on Sunday night, you decide something about your work.

Every time you swallow the truth one more time to keep the peace, you decide something about your relationships.

Every time you say, "I'm just tired," instead of, "I'm not living the way I want to live," you decide something about your future.

The question is no longer whether you are at a crossroads. The question is whether you will admit that you are—and act accordingly.

An invitation at the end of the road

So, here at the end of this book, the road narrows to something very simple and very difficult:

You have seen enough to know that continuing exactly as you are is not neutral. You have felt the ache of watching your own life from the edge of the room. You have glimpsed, in other people's stories and your own, the person you could be if you stopped postponing yourself.

The final tale is not written on these pages. It is written in what you do next.

Choose one place where you have been drifting and decide so small it almost feels embarrassing—and then keep it. Choose one place where you have been disappearing, and let yourself be seen, even a little. Choose one place where you have been postponing, and trade "someday" for a specific date on a real calendar.

You do not need to turn your life into a movie. You do not need a prophecy, a perfect plan, or a dramatic exit. You need a series of honest decisions that align your outer life with the self you have remembered while reading.

The tales of the self will continue long after you close this book. Thresholds will keep appearing in the ordinary corridors of your days—at the kitchen sink, in the meeting you dread, in the message you have not answered, in the mirror you avoid.

When they do, may something in you recognize the feel of them. May you pause, even for a breath, and remember that you are not just a character being carried along by the plot. You are the one who chooses.

And the choices you make—especially the quiet, unseen ones—are what will turn your life from a story you watched into a story you lived.

About the Author

Jorge Armenteros is an author who writes about the quiet moments where people begin to notice their own lives again. His work is shaped less by theory than by years of listening, watching, and observing how people drift, adapt, endure, and slowly recognize themselves.

Tales of the Self reflects a personal line of inquiry—an exploration of how easily we lose touch with the lives we are living, and how gently that connection can be restored.

He lives in Florida.

www.ingramcontent.com/pod-product-compliance
Lightning Source LLC
Chambersburg PA
CBHW020226130626
46549CB00005B/1763